Ribbon and Paint
Embroideries

RIBBON AND PAINT
Embroideries
ROSLYNN HAQ

SALLYMILNER
PUBLISHING

First published in 2003 by
Sally Milner Publishing Pty Ltd
PO Box 2104
Bowral NSW 2576
AUSTRALIA

© Roslynn Haq 2003

Design: Anna Warren, Warren Ventures
Editing: Sylvia Kalan
Photography: Tim Connolly

Printed in China

National Library of Australia Cataloguing-in-Publication data:

Haq, Roslynn.
   Ribbon and paint embroideries.

   ISBN 1 86351 321 3.

   1. Embroidery. 2. Ribbon work. I. Title. (Series : Milner craft series).

   746.44

10 9 8 7 6 5 4 3 2 1

CONTENTS

Acknowledgements

A very big thank you to Sally Milner Publishing for giving me the opportunity to publish this book, especially Libby Renney and Gabrielle Canny for their help and suggestions.

To my family, thank you for your support and encouragement always. Zareena, for her interest and Leila, for all the typing. Sarah and Ayesha for their graphics ideas. Siraj for his patience, suggestions and willingness to try out stitches! Bill, our dog, for his company under the table while I stitch and write.

Dedicated to Siraj.

INTRODUCTION

The use of ribbon for embroidery is a relatively late addition to the much earlier use of cotton, wool and silk. While these earlier materials were very much in functional use before becoming fashionable as decorative statements, ribbon embroidery has mainly flourished in its decorative form alone. More recently however, with the advent of rayon embroidery ribbon, it has been increasingly adapted for practical uses.

Ribbon embroidery offers a unique challenge to the creative mind, not seen in other forms of embroidery. The ribbon is an 'uncooperative' medium when compared to cotton threads and wool, and therefore inviting to be tamed. Two embroiderers engaged in the same project are quite likely to produce a similar but never identical result. Even when I stitch the same project twice, I can hardly ever duplicate it with any exactness.

The use of paint adds a further dimension to ribbon embroidery. The use of colour and a paint brush at the completion of the embroidery creates an opportunity to mimic the style of a painter, albeit on ribbon instead of canvas or paper. You have a chance to reproduce colours and shades in their most natural form, flowing ever so beautifully to catch the imagination. The result is what can aptly be described as an embroiderer's painting, worthy of framing or display in an exhibition.

When I first started experimenting with ribbon embroidery there were very few books to refer to and I soon learnt that there were equally few, if any, established rules to follow. This had great appeal to me as I have always had a nonconformist streak. Here was an art form that I could let my creative talent run wild with, not bound by convention. I could create new and different stitches and add colour through novel techniques.

Ribbon embroidery is also inherently untidy in its finished form and that too is different to other embroidery forms, where neatness and precision are the order of the day. However the results achieved with ribbon embroidery are, if anything, more naturally eye catching and skillful.

I regularly refer to gardening books for reference when starting on a new design involving flowers. Some of the best I have used are—

The Ultimate Book of Flowers for Australian Gardeners, by Rogar Mann,
     published by Random House for Lifetime distributors;
The Field Guide to Australian Wildflowers, by Denise Greig, published by New
     Holland;
Growing Fuchsias, by Deborah Law, published by Kangaroo Press;
Australia's Wildflowers Transforming the Landscape, by Denise Greig, published
     by New Holland.

The use of ginger jars in two of my projects was influenced by Malaysian
artist, Tang Yee Chuan, who has successfully and quite stunningly combined
paintings of blue and white pottery with pieces of fabric in his mixed collage
work. The combination of fabric, thread and embellishments adds another
interesting dimension to the limitless world of ribbon embroidery.

   The aim for my designs has been to extend my own and others, often
undiscovered, embroidery and artistic skills. I encourage experimentation and
diversity, aim to be bold about trying something new and making it work.

   Whilst teaching embroidery over the years, I have noticed that a student's
time has become more and more precious. Most find little time for leisure
and pleasure because of work and family pressures.

   I really dislike unfinished projects and have become aware of the increasing
numbers owned by many embroiderers. These invariably result from
complex, time-consuming classes where the expectation is that the stitcher has
little else to fill the day. With this in mind, I set about designing achievable
projects, where the end is definitely in sight, and much embroidery pleasure is
to be had along the way.

   Being almost entirely self-taught and often working in isolation from other
embroidery styles, necessity has definitely been the mother of invention for
me. Cost and easy availability of materials has always been utmost in my
mind. To this end I have designed my projects to be stitched in most brands
of embroidery ribbons and threads, in readily available colours. It is not
necessary to buy a multitude of differing colours as the ribbons can be hand
coloured once the embroidery is completed. This also gives a more realistic
distribution of colour on petals and leaves, which is otherwise quite difficult
to achieve with ribbon.

   I have included detailed instructions on framing your completed projects.

This valuable information will expand your skills, is much more economic and removes the need to send your embroidery masterpiece away for framing.

It has always been my very great pleasure to share ideas and help many embroiderers with the first steps. I hope that through this book many more will find the same enjoyment and satisfaction in what is easily possible.

Happy stitching!

GETTING STARTED

Fabrics. A wide range of fabrics, both plain and patterned, is suitable as backgrounds for most ribbon embroidery projects. Medium-weight fabrics are ideal. Fine, light-weight fabrics require a little more effort with finishing off the ribbon ends, as they can show through to the right side of the fabric. Some stretch fabrics are difficult to use because of a certain amount of 'give' in the fabric that makes it hard to pull the needle and ribbon through. It is worth persevering though, as ribbon embroidery on stretch fabrics, such as a windcheater or jacket, looks great. Take care when pulling the needle and ribbon through the fabric to minimize any uneven stretch of the fabric.

Embroidery ribbons. In this book mostly 4mm (³⁄₁₆") and 7mm (⁵⁄₁₆") ribbons are used, with a few 25mm (1") ribbons for big leaves in the larger projects. Almost all of the projects are worked in Mokuba and Sillook rayon ribbon. This is particularly suited to embroidery on clothing, as it is strong, handles well and the colours do not fade or run when washed. It is also readily available in a large range of colours. Beginners find the rayon a little easier to handle than silk and less expensive when starting out. Silk, satin and wired ribbons are also useful for different flowers and effects.

Needles. For most ribbon embroidery, a size 20 or 22 chenille needle is suitable, with a size 18 chenille best for wider ribbon. The sharp point and long wide eye of the chenille needle makes an ideal size hole in the fabric for the sometimes bulky ribbon to follow through. A chenille 22 can also be used for six strands of stranded cotton or for perlé threads.

- A crewel 8 needle should be used when stitching with fine threads, and one or two strands of stranded cotton.

- A straw or milliner's needle with its small eye and long shaft is ideal for bullion stitches. Use sizes 1–4 for four to six strands of stranded cotton and sizes 5-8 for one to four strands.

Embroidery hoops. Some embroiderers, in particular beginners, find a hoop helpful. It does tend to make checking the back of the work easier and keeps the working surface at the front smooth and taut. I prefer to embroider without a hoop and find that stitches worked in a scooping motion are generally more easily worked without a hoop. Stitch the way that best suits you. It all tends to be a matter of personal preference.

Paint. For flowers with more than one colour on their petals or leaves, painting after completion of the embroidery can produce dramatic effects. Silk paint is available at specialist silk painting outlets, some larger craft outlets and art material shops. Only very small amounts are required for the projects in this book as silk paint tends to be expensive. Many people have attempted silk painting and have paint left over which is ideal for use when painting ribbon embroidery.

Food colouring also works well to colour ribbons. This is readily available from cake decorating shops in a wide range of colours, with a lesser range in supermarkets. Silk paint and food colouring will mix together to obtain a desired shade.

Watercolour pencils. These beautiful, useful pencils have been used to colour the ginger jars in two projects. They can be used dry or, for more intense colour, with water. A little practice is required for best results. Several brands are available in art shops, some toy shops and newsagents. Some art supplies shops have a wide range of colours sold as individual pencils.

Fabric painting pens. The outlines of the designs on the ginger jars used in this book are drawn with fabric painting pens. These are generally available at larger craft outlets and art supplies stores. They have a brush like tip and a smaller tip, making them ideal for drawing lines of differing thickness. Pigma pens are also recommended for drawing very fine permanent lines.

Double sided fuseable webbing, e.g. Vliesofix, which is usually used for appliqué, has been used in projects that require fabric or braids to be fixed to background fabrics.

Care of embroidery and ribbon embroidery with painted finishes. Unpainted embroidery ribbon, particularly rayon will wash well and is very strong even if repeatedly machine washed. Particular care will need to be taken with painted ribbon as it is not washable. Finished ribbon embroidery should never be ironed, as once flattened the ribbon will have lost its three dimensional effect, never to be regained.

As with most other embroidery, ribbon embroidery should not be hung in direct sunlight as some fading could be expected if continually exposed to bright light.

RIBBON EMBROIDERY SAMPLERS

The four samplers included in this book will appeal to embroiderers with varying levels of embroidery skills.

The Summer Sampler is suited to all levels of embroiderers and for absolute beginners in ribbon embroidery who have basic embroidery skills.

The Autumn Sampler and Australian Wildflower Sampler are good follow on projects. The flowers in the Spring Sampler are a little more challenging, but not difficult.

All sections of each sampler can be worked individually and can make ideal small gifts. They do not take long to complete and could be framed individually and hung in groups.

Summer Sampler

MATERIALS

Dark green velvet 34cm x 30cm
 (13½" x 12")
Medium thickness craft wadding 34cm x 30cm
 (13½" x 12")
Medium to heavy-weight non iron-on
 interfacing 34cm x 30cm (13½" x 12")
Dark green machine thread

Embroidery ribbon 4mm (³/₁₆")
10 shades of pink from very pale to dark
 dusky pinks
Burgundy
Pale lemon
Pale butter lemon
Ivory
White
Lavender — dark, medium and pale
Very pale blue/green
Pale blue/green
Light olive green
Mid brown

Embroidery ribbon 7mm (⁵/₁₆")
6 shades of pink from very pale to burgundy
Pale lemon
Ivory
Dark lavender
Light olive green
Olive green
Dark blue/green

Medium blue/green
Dark green
Pale butter yellow

Stranded cottons
Dark burgundy
Rose pink
Dark plum
Gold
Pale lemon
Lemon
Pale green
Mid green
Pale blue/green
Medium blue/green
Dark blue/green
White

Perlé No. 5 cotton
Dark lavender
Medium lavender
Light blue/green
Medium blue/green

Perlé No. 8 cotton
Very pale green

Needles
Chenille 20 or 22 for ribbon
Crewel for stranded cotton and perlé

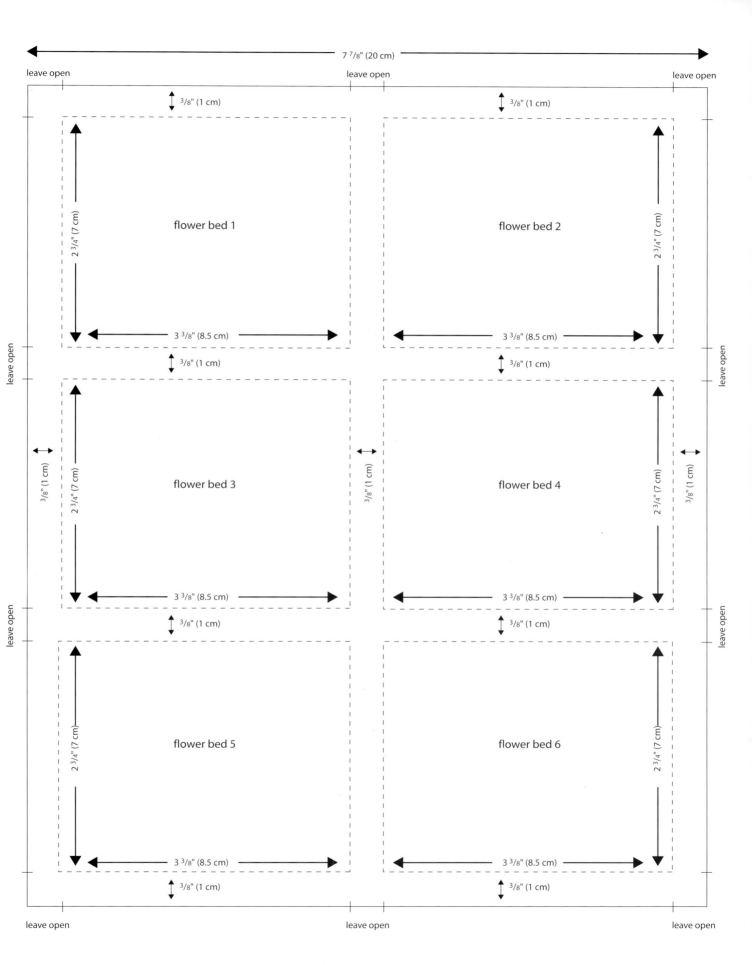

diagram 1 (enlarge at 110% on a photocopier)

STITCHES USED

Detached chain stitch

French knot

Colonial knot

Ribbon stitch

Straight stitch

Looped ribbon stitch

Pistil stitch

Stem stitch

Measurements for the six garden beds

See Diagram 1

To construct the garden beds

Using the cut piece of interfacing and the measurements set out in diagram 1, draw or trace the boxes with a sharp pencil or ball point pen.

Place the velvet right side down and then place the piece of wadding on top of the velvet.

Place the piece of marked interfacing on top of the wadding and pin around the outer edges. Tack all three pieces together.

With dark green machine thread and the stitch length at its longest setting, machine stitch along the marked lines on the interfacing to form six individual garden beds. Leave openings on each of the four outer corners, on each side of the two central channels and the centre channel, as shown in diagram 1. When the embroidery is completed these channels are filled with small amounts of fiberfill to form raised edges for each garden bed.

Overlock, zigzag or tape the edges with masking tape to stop the background fabric from fraying whilst the embroidery is being stitched.

Flower Bed 1

Pansies and Tulips

See Diagram 2

Diagram 2

Stitch the three pansies in straight stitch using 7mm (⁵⁄₁₆") ribbon. Use three different shades of pink for the upper petals, ivory for the central flower's lower petals and pale lemon for the lower petals of both outer flowers. For each petal, embroider straight stitches from side to side in the order indicated in diagram 3(a). The number of petals in each pansy will vary according to the look and fullness of the flower required. Work from the outside edge of each petal towards the centre. Leave a space in the centre of each flower for a colonial knot worked in very pale blue/green 4mm (³⁄₁₆") ribbon as shown in diagram 3 (b).

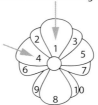 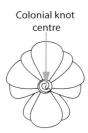

Diagram 3a   *Diagram 3b*

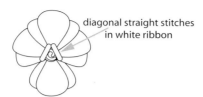

diagonal straight stitches
in white ribbon

Diagram 3c

Work the face of each pansy in straight stitch, using a single strand of dark burgundy stranded cotton on the middle and lower petals.

Add diagonal straight stitches to each petal in white 4mm (³⁄₁₆") ribbon as shown in diagram 3(c).

Embroider the leaves using light olive green and olive green 7mm (⁵⁄₁₆") ribbon with either detached chain or ribbon stitch.

Stitch the tulip stems with straight stitch using medium blue/green perlé 5 cotton. Embroider the petals in ribbon stitch with burgundy, pale butter yellow and ivory 4mm (³⁄₁₆") ribbon. Do not pull the ribbon stitches tightly to a point, leave a ruffled edge at the top of each flower.

Work the tulip leaves in very pale blue/green and pale blue/green 4mm (³⁄₁₆") ribbon using ribbon stitch.

Finish by stitching two long horizontal straight stitches at the base of the pansies in dark blue/green 7mm (⁵⁄₁₆") ribbon. With a single strand of matching stranded cotton, secure the two lengths of ribbon at each end with small slipstitches as shown in diagram 4.

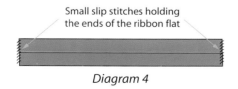

Small slip stitches holding
the ends of the ribbon flat

Diagram 4

Flower Bed 2

Daisies

See Diagram 5.

Diagram 5

Stitch the pink daisies in detached chains, some in 7mm (⁵⁄₁₆") and some in 4mm (³⁄₁₆") ribbon using six different shades of pink.

Start with the largest flowers in the centre of the bed. I like to work the petals and then the centres but some embroiderers find it easier to work the centres of the flowers first. Stitch the centres with groups of 3–5 wrap French knots in three to four strands of stranded cotton each, in pale green and mid green and pale lemon and lemon. Vary the number of knots used for each flower. Include partial flowers to fill any available spaces.

Embroider the leaves in light olive green and olive green ribbon, using both 7mm (⁵⁄₁₆") and 4mm (³⁄₁₆") ribbon, in either detached chain or ribbon stitch.

Flower Bed 3

Delphiniums, Foxgloves and Lilies
See Diagram 6.

Diagram 6

Embroider the stems for the three main flowers in three strands of mid-green stranded cotton using stem stitch, leaving space on each side of the central flower for the lilies.

Work the delphinium petals in looped ribbon stitch using dark lavender 7mm (⁵⁄₁₆") ribbon at the base of the stem, graduating to 4mm (³⁄₁₆") ribbon at the top of the stem. Add several single wrap French knots in pale lavender 4mm (³⁄₁₆") ribbon, then several in pale blue/green 4mm (³⁄₁₆") ribbon, according to the available spaces towards the top of the stem. Hold the looped ribbon stitch petals in place with a straight stitch loop using a single strand of dark blue/green stranded cotton.

Stitch the leaves with three long detached chains in medium blue/green 7mm (⁵⁄₁₆") ribbon.

To work the one ivory and one pale lemon foxglove, starting approximately 6mm (¼") down from the top of the stem, stitch the petals in ribbon stitch using 4mm (³⁄₁₆") ribbon, graduating to 7mm (⁵⁄₁₆") ribbon at the base of the flower. Do not pull the stitches to a point.

Add single wrap French knots in pale blue/green 4mm (³⁄₁₆") ribbon as for the delphiniums and some in ivory and pale lemon if space permits.

Embroider the leaves in long detached chain stitches in dark green 7mm (⁵⁄₁₆") ribbon.

Work the lilies in ribbon stitch using ivory 7mm (⁵⁄₁₆") ribbon with 3–4 wrap pistil stitch centres in two strands of gold stranded cotton. Add the stems in straight stitch using very pale green perlé 8 cotton.

Embroider the lily leaves in ribbon stitch pulled firmly to a point in olive green 7mm (⁵⁄₁₆") ribbon.

Flower Bed 4

Lavender
See Diagram 7

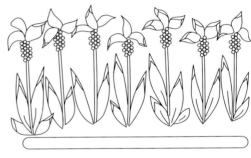

Diagram 7

Work seven stems of differing lengths in straight stitch using medium blue/green perlé 5 thread. Stitch colonial knots at the top of each stem in perlé 5 thread. Work four stems with knots in dark lavender and three in medium lavender.

Embroider the petals at the top of the knots in ribbon stitch using matching dark or medium lavender 4mm (³⁄₁₆") ribbon.

Stitch the leaves in ribbon stitch in very pale blue/green and pale blue/green 4mm (³⁄₁₆") ribbon.

Place a long straight stitch of mid brown 4mm (³⁄₁₆") ribbon at the base of the leaves.

Flower bed 5

Fuchsia

See Diagram 8.

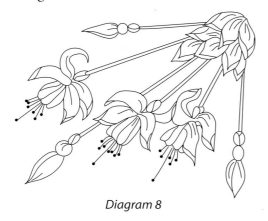

Diagram 8

Stitch six straight stitch stems of varying lengths, radiating from the top right hand corner, in medium blue/green perlé 5 cotton.

On the flower end of the stems, using pale blue/green 4mm (³⁄₁₆") ribbon, work one small straight stitch on each side of the stem.

Stitch the three flowers, two in deep rose pink and one in burgundy 4mm (³⁄₁₆") ribbon. Embroider loose straight stitches of the base of the flower as the corolla as shown in diagram 9a.

Diagram 9a

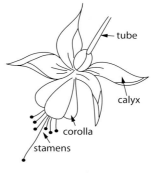

Diagram 9b

Work the centre petal first, stitching from the base of the flower up towards the stem, leaving space to add the calyx.

Stitch the calyx in pale pink 7mm (⁵⁄₁₆") ribbon in ribbon stitch worked loosely, allowing the ribbon to twist.

Following diagram 9b, stitch the stamen at the base of the flower in single strands of dark plum and rose pink stranded cotton in straight stitch, with a longer centre stamen in white stranded cotton. Finish off each stamen with a 2 wrap French knot using a single strand of matching stranded cotton.

Work the buds with two straight stitches in pink 7mm (⁵⁄₁₆") ribbon. Start on each side of the two small green straight stitches at the base of the stem, then enter the fabric at the same point for both stitches, forming stitches approximately 1.5cm (⁵⁄₈") in length as shown in diagram 10a.

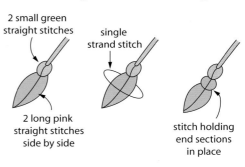

Diagrams 10a, b and c

Following diagram 10b, using a matching single strand of stranded cotton, approximately one third the way down the pink straight stitches, stitch across the ribbon horizontally from behind the stitches. Pull firmly, gathering the ribbon to form the shape of the bud as shown in diagram 10c.

Flower Bed 6

Poppies
See Diagram 11.

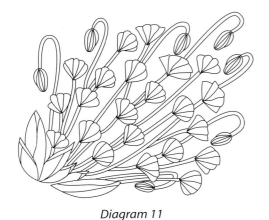

Diagram 11

Embroider the stems for the full flowers in straight stitch using light blue/green perlé 5 cotton and the stems for the buds in two strands of pale blue/green stranded cotton in stem stitch.

Work the petals in 4mm (³⁄₁₆") ribbon in dusty pink, pale pink, pale and medium lavender and pale lemon using straight stitch, starting from the outer edge of the flower and working in toward the centre. Keep the ribbon flat and free of twists. Add straight stitches of varying lengths at the base of each flower in two strands of dark blue/green stranded cotton, keeping the stitches in the shape of a fan.

Stitch the leaves in ribbon stitch using very pale blue/green and pale blue/green 4mm (³⁄₁₆") ribbon.

Add the buds as groups of straight stitches in three strands of medium blue/green stranded cotton.

On completion of the embroidery, using a satay stick, gently fill the machine stitched edges of the flower beds with craft wadding to give a raised edge to each bed. Using small straight running stitches in a matching thread, stitch the openings closed.

Spring Garden Sampler

MATERIALS

Dark green velvet 34cm x 30cm (13 ½" x 12")

Medium thickness craft wadding 34cm x 30cm (13 ½" x 12")

Medium-heavy non iron-on interfacing 34cm x 30cm (13 ½" x 12")

To prepare the flower beds follow the instructions for the 'Summer Sampler'.

Embroidery ribbon 4mm (³/₁₆")
White
Ivory
Pale lavender
Lavender
Dark purple
Deep rose pink
Gold
Butter yellow
Pale olive green
Olive green
Pale yellow/green
Very pale green
Very pale blue/green
Medium blue/green
Very dark blue/green
Brown

Embroidery ribbon 7mm (⁵/₁₆")
Lemon
Ivory

Pale lavender
Burgundy
Purple
Light blue/green
Medium blue/green
Very dark blue/green
Rayon ribbon 12mm (½")
Ivory

Silk ribbon 12mm (¹/₂")
Pale lemon

Stranded cottons
White
Pale blue/green
Medium dark blue/green
Pale yellow/green
Medium dark plum
Lemon

Perlé No.5 cotton
Dull yellow
Medium blue/green

Perlé No. 8 cotton
Dark green

Marlitt stranded rayon
Very pale green
Bright apple green

Needles

Chenille 20 or 22

Chenille 18 for 12mm (½") ribbon

Straw no.3 for bullion stitch

Straw no.7 for small bullion stitch

Crewel for stranded cotton

Sharp no.10 for gathering ribbon

Silk paint or food colouring

Yellow

Red

Blue

STITCHES USED

Straight stitch

Ribbon stitch

Stem stitch

Whipped stem stitch

Bullion stitch

Detached chain stitch

Blanket stitch

Flower Bed 1

Snowdrops

See Diagram 1.

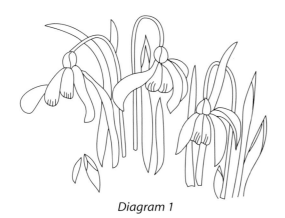

Diagram 1

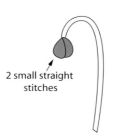

2 small straight stitches

Diagram 2

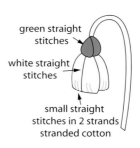

green straight stitches

white straight stitches

small straight stitches in 2 strands stranded cotton

Diagram 3

Embroider the three stems using two strands of pale blue/green stranded cotton. Work the lower two thirds of the stem's length in whipped chain stitch and change to stem stitch for the curved overhanging section of stem. Following diagram 2, using very pale green 4mm (³⁄₁₆") ribbon, work two small straight stitches at the end of each stem.

Following diagram 3, add three straight stitches in white 4mm (³⁄₁₆") ribbon, being careful not to pull the ribbon too tightly. On the lower tip of each of these stitches work several straight stitches in two strands of pale yellow/green stranded cotton. Following diagram 4, work three to four long loose straight stitches in white 4mm (³⁄₁₆") ribbon over the top of the first straight stitches, allowing some to twist a little. Couch in place with very small straight stitches using a single strand of white stranded cotton.

Embroider the leaves in three shades of blue/green 4mm (³⁄₁₆") ribbon using ribbon stitch pulled firmly to a point.

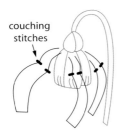

Diagram 4

one petal on each
side of the stem
ribbon stitch, leaving
a rolled edge

Diagram 6

Flower Bed 2

Tulips
See Diagram 5

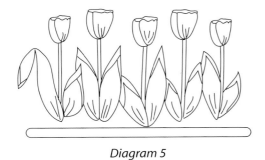

Diagram 5

Embroider five stems in medium blue/green perlé 5 cotton using straight stitch. With lemon, pale lavender, purple and burgundy 7mm (⁵⁄₁₆") ribbon and ribbon stitch, work the petals for each flower, placing one stitch on each side of the stem. Do not pull the stitches through to a point but leave a rolled edge as shown in diagram 6. Sometimes a third petal stitch may be required to fill any space in the centre of the flower.

Add two leaves to each flower using light blue/green 7mm (⁵⁄₁₆") ribbon, with each ribbon stitch pulled firmly to a point. Add a straight stitch facing downwards at an angle to the leaf to the left of the flowers as shown in diagram 7. This may be worked in light blue/green 7mm (⁵⁄₁₆") ribbon folded over, or in very pale blue/green 4mm (³⁄₁₆") ribbon.

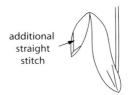

additional
straight
stitch

Diagram 7

Place a long horizontal straight stitch in brown 4mm (³⁄₁₆") ribbon, slightly below the completed flowers.

Painted Petals
Mix red and blue silk paint or food colouring to a dark purple shade. Paint a touch of colour on to the ivory and purple tulips using very small amounts of mixed paint. Always test the colour first on a scrap of ribbon. Add colour gradually and dry between coats using a hair dryer.

Flower Bed 3

Narcissus

See Diagram 8

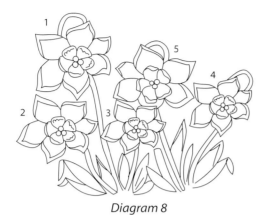

Diagram 8

Mark the position for the centre of each of the five flowers with a white marker pen or by stitching a cross stitch in white machine thread.

For flowers 1, 2, 3 and 4, work the outer petals in ribbon stitch using ivory 12mm (½") rayon ribbon and a number 18 chenille needle, leaving space in the centre for an inner round of petals as shown in diagram 9.

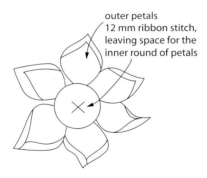

outer petals
12 mm ribbon stitch,
leaving space for the
inner round of petals

Diagram 9

Embroider the outer petals of flower 5 in pale lemon 12 mm (½") silk ribbons in the same manner as the other flowers.

For all flowers, stitch the inner petals in lemon 7mm (5⁄16") ribbon as shown in diagram 10. Do not pull the ribbon stitches through to a point, but leave with a rolled edge.

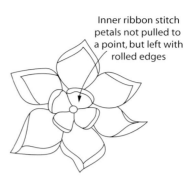

Inner ribbon stitch
petals not pulled to
a point, but left with
rolled edges

Diagram 10

Fill the centre of each flower with three to five colonial knots using dull yellow perlé 5 cotton.

Stitch the stems in long bullion knots using six strands of pale blue/green stranded cotton and a number 3 straw needle. The bullion will take 45–65 wraps, depending of the tightness of the wrapping. Complete the stems by adding curved bullion loops above flowers 1, 4 and 5 using four strands of pale blue/green stranded cotton. Work 12–16 wraps, couched if necessary to hold in place.

Embroider the leaves in pale olive green and olive green 4mm (3⁄16") ribbon in both detached chain and ribbon stitch, three with small straight stitch additions at the top.

Painted Petals

With a fine tipped paint brush, paint the outer petals of flowers 1 and 4 with undiluted yellow silk paint or food colouring. It may require several coats to get the required intensity of colour, especially on the tips of the petals.

Paint all the inner petals with a mixture of yellow and a very small touch of red silk paint or food colouring. Test the colours on a scrap of ribbon before painting the embroidery. Apply more intense colour to the rolled edges. With diluted green silk paint or food colouring, add a touch of green to the centre of the colonial knots, drying immediately with a hair dryer to prevent the colour spreading to the petals.

Flower Bed 4

Iris
See Diagram 11

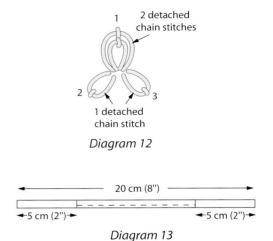

Diagram 12

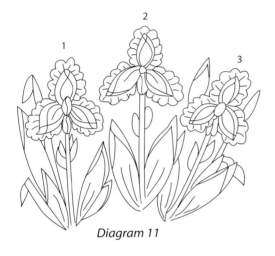

Diagram 11

Embroider three different length stems in double whipped stem stitch using six strands of medium dark blue/green stranded cotton, adding buds with two to four ribbon stitches in medium blue/green 4mm (³⁄₁₆") ribbon, to each stem. On flower 1, place gold 4mm (³⁄₁₆") ribbon straight stitches just above the green ribbon stitches, close to the stem.

At the uppermost tip of the stems, place a small straight stitch on each side of the stem in the same shade and width of ribbon as the buds.

For flower 1 and 2, stitch the inner petals in butter yellow 4mm (³⁄₁₆") ribbon, in detached chain. Fill in the centre of the detached chains with straight stitches. Place a second detached chain around the outer edge of the first stitch as shown in diagram 12.

Diagram 13

Embroider flower 3 in the same way as flowers 1 and 2 using dark purple 4mm (³⁄₁₆") ribbon.

Work frilled edges on flower 1 and 2 around the detached chain stitches using a 20cm (8") length of butter yellow 4mm (³⁄₁₆") ribbon. Using a single strand of matching cotton and starting 5cm (2") in from the cut edge, place small running stitches along one edge of the selvage to within 5cm (2") of the opposite edge as shown in diagram 13. Loosely gather the ribbon. Thread one end of the gathered ribbon into a chenille needle and take the tail to the back of the work at the base of the upper detached chain and secure. Repeat on the other side of the detached chain as shown in diagram 14. Pull up the gathers, and with small stitches in matching thread, stitch the gathered ribbon in place around the first detached chain. Repeat in the same manner for petals 2 and 3.

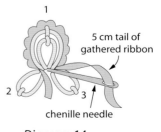

Diagram 14

Work flower 3 in the same manner, using deep rose pink for the frills around each of the detached chains.

Painted Petals

Mix together yellow and a little red silk paint or food colouring for flowers 1 and 2 and red and blue silk paint or food colouring for flower 3 and with a fine tipped paint brush, carefully add paint to the frills and detached chains. Dry immediately with a hair dryer.

Stitch the leaves in ribbon stitch using two shades of green, some in medium blue/green 7mm (⁵⁄₁₆") ribbon, and others in very dark blue/green 4mm (³⁄₁₆") ribbon. Add small straight stitches at the tip of some of the leaves.

Flower Bed 5

Wisteria
See Diagram 15

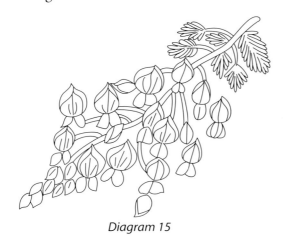

Diagram 15

Embroider the main stem in pale blue/green stranded cotton in three separate sections, starting from the top right hand corner of the garden bed as shown in diagram 16. Use six strands with a number 3 straw needle and a 60–70 wrap bullion knot.

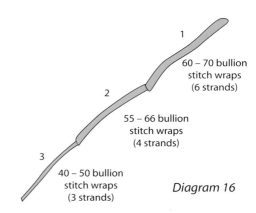

1

60 – 70 bullion
stitch wraps
(6 strands)

2

55 – 66 bullion
stitch wraps
(4 strands)

3

40 – 50 bullion
stitch wraps
(3 strands)

Diagram 16

Work the second section with four strands and a 55–65 wrap bullion knot, then the third section in the lower left hand corner of the flower bed in three strands and a 40–50 wrap bullion knot. Couch all sections in place with a single strand of matching thread.

Stitch three bullion knot stems for the leaves using three strands of pale yellow/green stranded cotton using 10–15 wraps for each leaf stem.

Work approximately ten stems for the flowers in medium dark plum stranded cotton, some using three strands and some two strands and 8–12 wrap bullion knots. Extra stems may need to be added after the flowers and buds are worked.

Randomly place thirteen to fourteen full flowers along the stems, with three placed across the stem where the bullion knots join. Following diagram 17a, work the upper petals with ivory 7mm (⁵⁄₁₆") ribbon using ribbon stitch. Place two stitches side by side, with the stitches pulled up to a point from the side of the ribbon rather than the centre, as shown in diagram 17b. To get the correct shape of these petals, it may be necessary to couch the corners of the lower edge of the petals in place with a single strand of matching thread as shown in diagram 17c.

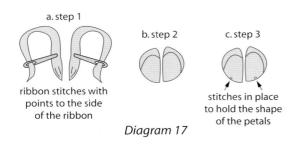

a. step 1

b. step 2

c. step 3

ribbon stitches with
points to the side
of the ribbon

stitches in place
to hold the shape
of the petals

Diagram 17

Using pale lavender 4mm (³⁄₁₆") ribbon, work two small ribbon stitches side by side for the lower petals. Pull these stitches through the same exit point to the back of the fabric as shown in diagram 18.

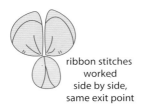

ribbon stitches
worked
side by side,
same exit point

Diagram 18

Stitch the larger buds closest to the leaves in lavender 4mm (³⁄₁₆") ribbon with two ribbon stitches worked side by side. Embroider the remaining buds with small ribbon stitches randomly placed. Add a few very pale green 4mm (³⁄₁₆") ribbon stitches towards the lower end of the stem.

Embroider the six leaves using a single strand of very pale green Marlitt in detached chain in graduating lengths, as shown in diagram 19.

detached chain
leaves

start

Diagram 19

Painted Petals

Mix together red and blue silk paint or food colouring, adding lots of water to dilute to a pale shade of purple. With a fine tipped paint brush, paint the upper tips of the two large petals, adding a little paint to the outer edges of the petals. Dry immediately with a hair dryer to halt the spread of the paint. On some of the lower petals add a little purple paint and dry with a hair dryer.

Mix yellow silk paint or food colouring with water to a pale lemon. Carefully apply to the centre of the two large petals, just above the two small ribbon stitch petals and dry immediately.

Paint the tips of some of the buds with the same purple as for the petals. If a darker shade is required, add more paint gradually, drying between coats.

Flower Bed 6

Angel Trumpets

See Diagram 20.

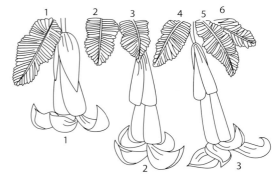

Diagram 20

Using medium blue/green perlé 5 cotton, place three straight stitches of differing lengths immediately below the upper edge of the flower bed. Place one stem approximately 15mm (⅝") long to the right of the garden bed, one 10mm (⅜") to the left and one in the centre, 12mm (½") long.

Stitch leaves 1, 3, 4 and 5 in dark green perlé 8 cotton and leaf 2 in two single strands of bright apple green Marlitt. Embroider leaf 6 in a single strand of bright apple green Marlitt. Stitch the leaves in blanket stitch, with the central vein in stem stitch as shown in diagram 21. Start the blanket stitch from the tip of the leaves, working each side of the leaf separately and keeping the stitches close together.

Diagram 21

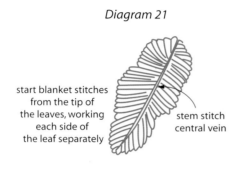

start blanket stitches from the tip of the leaves, working each side of the leaf separately

stem stitch central vein

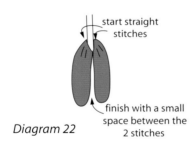

start straight stitches

finish with a small space between the 2 stitches

Diagram 22

Following diagram 22 and using very dark blue/green 7mm (⁵⁄₁₆") ribbon, work two long straight stitches, placing a stitch on each side of the base of the stem and finishing about two needles width away from each other. Keep the ribbon flat and free from twists.

Following diagram 23a, embroider the flowers with two to three straight stitches in ivory 7mm (⁵⁄₁₆") ribbon for flower 1 and ivory 4mm (³⁄₁₆") ribbon for flowers 2 and 3. Start in the space between the green straight stitches as shown in diagram 23b.

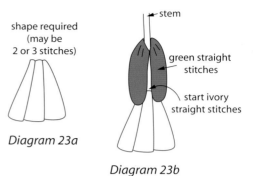

shape required (may be 2 or 3 stitches)

stem

green straight stitches

start ivory straight stitches

Diagram 23a

Diagram 23b

Embroider the lower petals in ivory 7mm (⁵⁄₁₆") ribbon using ribbon stitch, keeping these stitches loose and allow to twist as shown in diagram 24.

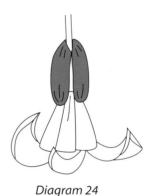

Diagram 24

Painted Petals

With silk paint or food colouring, mix tiny amounts of yellow and red paint with water, testing the shades on a scrap of ribbon. Apply the very palest of pink paint with a fine brush to the top of the long ivory straight stitches just below the green straight stitches on flowers 1 and 2. Apply a stronger shade of the same colour to flower 3. Paint the stronger shade onto the lower petals of this flower, particularly towards the petal's tips.

Mix blue and yellow colouring with lots of water to a very pale dull green. Apply sparingly to the ivory straight stitches just below the green straight stitches. Dry with a hair dryer.

Autumn Sampler

MATERIALS

Dark green velvet 34cm x 30cm (13½" x 12")

Medium thickness craft wadding 34cm x 30cm (13½" x 12")

Very small amount of fiberfill

Medium-heavy weight non iron on interfacing 34cm x 30cm (13½" x 12")

Dark green machine thread

The instructions for tracing and constructing the flower beds for this project are the same as those for the 'Summer Sampler' on page 18.

Embroidery ribbon 4mm (³/₁₆")

Red — two shades
Orange
Brown
Pale lemon
Deep purple
Dark purple
Very dark purple
Gold
Dark olive green
Light blue/green
Sage green
Very pale green
White
Dark plum
Mid plum
Dusty pink
Light beige

Embroidery ribbon 7mm (⁵/₁₆")

Dark blue/green
Mid green
Dark green

Wired 25mm (1") ribbon

Yellow
Orange

Hand-dyed Hannah 25mm (1") ribbon

Green

Stranded cottons

Dark brown
Mid brown
Fawn
Light beige
Dark straw
White
Red
Butter yellow
Deep lemon
Burgundy
Black
Dark green
Light blue/green
Medium blue/green

Perlé no. 5 cotton

Light beige
Gold

Perlé no. 3 cotton

Lemon

Gold

Needles

Chenille 20 or 22 for ribbon work

Crewel for stranded and perlé cotton

Straw no. 3 for bullion knots

Red and yellow silk paint or food colouring

Available from art supplies shops, supermarkets and specialty cake decorating shops.

STITCHES USED

Whipped stem stitch

Ribbon stitch

Straight stitch

Stem stitch

Colonial knot

French knot

Bullion knot

Whipped chain stitch

Fly stitch

Fly stitch leaves

Blanket stitch

Flower Bed 1
Red Berries
See Diagram 1

Embroider the main stem in whipped stem stitch. Work the stem stitch in four strands of mid brown stranded cotton and whip those stitches with three strands of dark brown stranded cotton.

Stitch the stems for the berries in either two strands of fawn or two shades of brown stranded cotton using stem stitch.

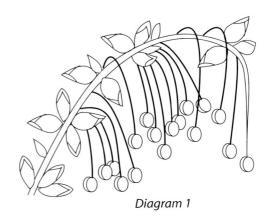

Diagram 1

Diagram 2

Work the berries in two shades of red, orange and dark purple 4mm (³⁄₁₆") ribbon. Stitch each berry with one colonial knot with 2-3 straight stitches worked over the top of the knot as shown in diagram 2. The number of straight stitches will vary according to the shape and size of the berry required. Do not pull the stitches too tightly. Finish the straight stitches at the same point at the base of the berry. Highlight some berries with a small straight stitch using two strands of white stranded cotton.

Using either dark green 7mm (⁵⁄₁₆") ribbon or dark olive green 4mm (³⁄₁₆") ribbon, embroider the leaves in ribbon stitch working two stitches for each leaf sitting side by side.

Colouring

Mix the yellow and red silk paint or food colouring to make brown. Paint the tips of the dark olive green leaves. Dry immediately with a hair dryer.

Flower Bed 2

Daisies
See Diagram 3

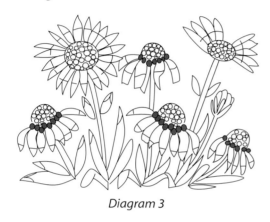

Diagram 3

Embroider the stems for the daisies in bullion knots using six strands of two shades of blue/green stranded cotton. Vary the length of the stems between 50–75 wrap bullion knots. An alternative stitch for the stems which also looks good is whipped stem stitch using six strands of light and medium blue/green stranded cotton.

Stitch the petals of the full and partial daisies in pale lemon and gold 4mm (³⁄₁₆") ribbon using ribbon stitch. For each full daisy work the flower centre in colonial knots in four strands of butter yellow and dark straw stranded cotton. For the partial flowers, embroider brown knot centres with black knots on the edges near the petals and add small, looped straight stitches in deep lemon stranded cotton·in a single strand between some of the brown knots.

Embroider the bud using straight stitch in pale lemon 4mm (³⁄₁₆") ribbon. Work foliage on the petals close to the stem in straight stitch in four strands of blue/green stranded cotton, matching the green to that used on the stem.

Add the leaves in light blue/green and sage green 4mm (³⁄₁₆") ribbon with long and short ribbon stitch.

Colouring

On completion of the embroidery, paint the daisy petals with silk paint or food colouring. Mix red with water to produce dark pink and then light pink. If colouring ribbon for the first time, it is worth embroidering several practice flowers and to use these to test the colours mixed. Build up the colour gradually and dry with a hair dryer between applications. Add light pink to the outer edge of the petals of the full daisy and the upper partial daisy and dark pink to the inner edge of the remaining petals.

Flower Bed 3

Yellow Yarrow
See Diagram 4

Diagram 4

Embroider the stems for the three large yarrow flowers with 40–55 wrap bullion knots in six strands of dark straw stranded cotton. If preferred, the stems may also be worked in whipped chain stitch.

Stitch the stems for the two smaller flowers in whipped stem stitch in two strands of light beige stranded cotton. Add small stems between the flowers and the main stem using light beige perlé 5 cotton in straight stitch.

Embroider the flowers in orange, gold, lemon and light beige 4mm (³⁄₁₆") ribbon and perlé 5 and perlé 3 in light beige, gold and lemon.

Add the leaves in dark blue/green 7mm (⁵⁄₁₆") and light blue/green 4mm (³⁄₁₆") ribbon with long and short ribbon stitch.

Place one long horizontal straight stitch at the base of the flowers and leaves in brown 4mm (³⁄₁₆") ribbon, couching in place if necessary with matching thread.

Flower Bed 4

Chinese Lanterns
See Diagram 5.

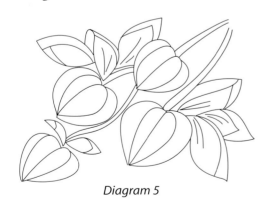

Diagram 5

Construct the Chinese Lantern pods with yellow and orange 25mm (1") wired ribbon. On completion of the stitching add colour to the pods with silk paint or food colouring. For each pod cut a 12cm (5") length of wired ribbon. Following diagram 6, fold the ribbon in half and with matching thread and using very small running stitches, stitch through both thicknesses of the ribbon starting from the fold at the selvage edges. Work across the ribbon, curving up to the top selvage edge and finishing at the cut edge of the ribbon.

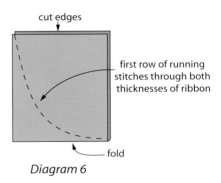

Diagram 6

Open out the ribbon, make a small fold on each side of the first row of running stitches, half way between these stitches and the selvage edges. With small running stitches, stitch down the length of each fold and across at the lower edge to meet the point at the base of the first row of stitches, as shown in diagram 7.

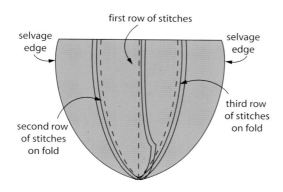

Diagram 7

Fold the wide end of the ribbon over to form the top of the pod near the stems.

Position each Chinese Lantern pod on the flower bed and pin in place. Insert a small amount of fiberfill stuffing under each pod to give fullness. Slipstitch each pod in place, using double threaded invisible thread or a single strand of matching stranded cotton.

Embroider the stems with long bullion knots using six strands of dark straw stranded cotton. The number of wraps will vary with the length of stem required. Allow the stems to sit over the edge of an adjoining pod. Couch in place with matching thread.

Stitch the large leaves using ribbon stitch in green Hannah 25mm (1") ribbon. Add small ribbon stitch leaves in mid green 7mm (⁵⁄₁₆") ribbon.

Colouring

On completion of the embroidery add extra colour to the pods with silk paint or food colouring. Mix red and yellow to achieve a deep orange and deep gold. Paint the deep orange on to the orange pods and the deep gold to the yellow pods. Also add small touches of pale green sparingly to the yellow pods. Add the colour sparingly, drying with a hair dryer between each application.

Flower Bed 5

Blackberries

See Diagram 8

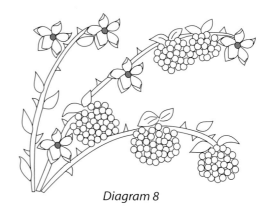

Diagram 8

Stitch the three stems with whipped stem stitch using four strands of stranded cotton, combining two strands of dark green and two strands of burgundy in the needle.

Add the berries in colonial knots and 3–4 wrap French knots using deep purple, dark purple, very dark purple and dark plumb, mid plumb and sage green 4mm (³⁄₁₆") ribbon. Vary the placing of the knots to produce a different look to each berry.

For the flowers, ribbon stitch the petals in white 4mm (³⁄₁₆") ribbon and add colonial knot centers in dark olive green 4mm (³⁄₁₆") ribbon.

Randomly place small leaves in very pale green 4mm (³⁄₁₆") ribbon using ribbon stitch along the stems, adding several other ribbon stitches where space permits in sage green 4mm (³⁄₁₆") ribbon.

Embroider thorns in two strands of red stranded cotton with fly stitch adding a straight stitch in the centre.

Flower Bed 6

Variegated leaves

See Diagram 9

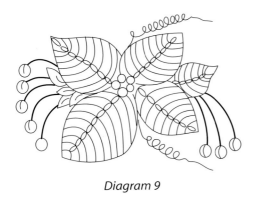

Diagram 9

Embroider the four central berries in dark red 4mm (³⁄₁₆") ribbon and one in sage green 4mm (³⁄₁₆") ribbon using colonial knots with straight stitches worked over the knots to form a rounded shape.

Stitch the leaves in fly stitch in sage green, very pale green, pale lemon, gold and orange 4mm (³⁄₁₆") ribbon, working approximately two stitches per colour. Outline each leaf with small blanket stitch around the outer edges using a single strand of red stranded cotton.

Embroider the stems for the outer berries in stem stitch using two strands of mid brown, dark brown and fawn stranded cotton.

Add the berries at the end of the stems with 4mm (³⁄₁₆") ribbon, stitching two red, one gold and one sage green in colonial knots covered with straight stitches.

Fill in the spaces with small ribbon stitch leaves in dark olive green 4mm (³⁄₁₆") ribbon.

Add tendrils using a single strand of light beige stranded cotton. Wind the cotton firmly onto a satay stick, spray with hair spray until the thread is wet and allow to dry. When dry, carefully remove the stick and couch in place.

Australian Wildflower Sampler

MATERIALS

Dark green velvet 34cm x 30cm (13½" x 12")

Medium thickness craft wadding 34cm x 30cm
(13½" x 12")

Medium to heavy weight non iron on
interfacing 34cm x 30cm (13½" x 12")

Dark green machine thread

Construct the flower beds for this project
following the instructions set out in the
'Summer Sampler' on page 18.

Embroidery ribbon 4mm (³/₁₆")

Very pale green

Pale blue/green

Medium blue/green

Medium dark green

Dark pine green

Red – two shades

Black

Pale lemon

Lemon

Embroidery ribbon 7mm (⁵/₁₆")

Mid blue/green

Olive green

Lemon

Pale blue/green

Stranded cottons

Very pale blue/green

Light blue/green

Blue/green

Light olive green

White

Bright yellow

Brown

Silk threads

Deep rose pink

Red

Lemon

Brown

Appleton 2ply crewel wool

Lemon

Gold

DMC tapestry wool

Brown

Mill Hill glass seed beads

Yellow

7 x 6mm (¼") beads for gum nuts

Toothbrush

Needles

Chenille 20 or 22

Crewel for stranded cotton

Beading needle

STITCHES USED

Whipped chain stitch

Detached chain stitch

Straight stitch

Turkey or Ghiordes knot

Ribbon stitch

Couching

Stem stitch

Colonial knot

French knot

Fly stitch

Pistil stitch

Double whipped chain stitch

Flower Bed 1

Wattle
See Diagram 1

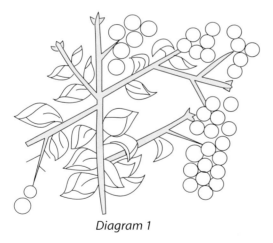

Diagram 1

Embroider the large stems in six strands of very pale blue/green stranded cotton with whipped chain stitch. Using three strands of the same thread, add three very small detached chain stitches to the tips of some of the stems.

Stitch the thinner stems in whipped chain stitch using two strands of very pale blue/green stranded cotton.

Add the blossom with gold and lemon wool in turkey knots, trimmed and brushed with a tooth brush until fluffy.

Randomly place the leaves in pale blue/green 7mm (5⁄16") and pale blue/green 4mm (3⁄16") ribbon using ribbon stitch.

Flower Bed 2

Gum Leaves and Gum Nuts
See Diagram 2

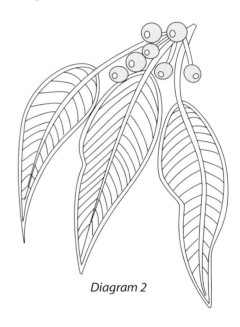

Diagram 2

Embroider the three leaf stems in four strands of blue/green stranded cotton using whipped chain stitch and outline the lower edges in two strands of brown stranded cotton using stem stitch.

To embroider the leaves, outline the shape of the each with a white marker pen. Work the centre leaf and the leaf to its left in medium blue/green 4mm (3⁄16") ribbon in straight stitch, keeping each stitch as flat as possible. Work the leaf to the right in the same manner using very pale green 4mm (3⁄16") ribbon. Stitch a central vein for each leaf in stem stitch in three strands of matching stranded cotton. Couch three strands of brown stranded cotton around the outline of each leaf.

To work each gum nut, double thread and knot the brown silk thread and wrap around a 6mm (¼") bead to cover completely. At one end, leave several tails of thread and blanket stitch over the threads to form a stalk. Attach each gum nut to the fabric, taking the stalk to the back of the fabric and finishing off securely.

Flower Bed 3

Sturt Desert Pea
See Diagram 3

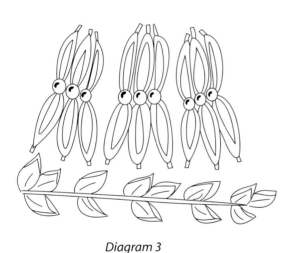

Diagram 3

Embroider the petals, starting with the upper central petals of the middle flower. Work long detached chain stitches in two shades of red 4mm (³⁄₁₆") ribbon. Stitch three upper and three lower petals. Fill the centres of the detached chains with straight stitches.

Work three to four colonial knots in black 4mm (³⁄₁₆") ribbon to form the centre of each

berry and cover with two to three straight stitches to form the rounded shape. Add white highlight straight stitches to each berry in a single strand of white stranded cotton.

Stitch the long stem for the leaves in six strands of very pale blue/green stranded cotton with whipped chain stitch.

Ribbon stitch the leaves in two shades of mid blue/green 7mm (⁵⁄₁₆") ribbon.

Flower Bed 4

Beaufortia
See Diagram 4

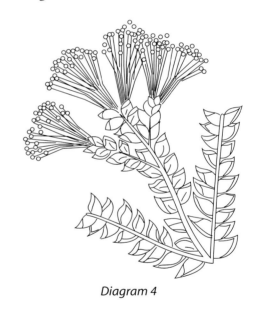

Diagram 4

Embroider the three main stems in whipped chain stitch using six strands of light olive green stranded cotton. Add four smaller stems using four strands of light olive green stranded cotton in whipped chain stitch.

Work the leaves in pairs using olive green 7mm (⁵⁄₁₆") ribbon in ribbon stitch on the three main stems. On the tip of each of the smaller stems, work several straight stitches in lemon 7mm (¾₆") and pale lemon 4mm (¾₆") ribbon.

Below the lemon straight stitches work pairs of ribbon stitch leaves in medium dark green 4mm (¾₆") ribbon. Above the lemon straight stitches, work groups of straight stitches in single strands of deep rose pink and red silk thread. Add longer straight stitches above the first group of straight stitches using the same silk threads.

Randomly work 3 wrap French knots on the tips of the longer straight stitches in a single strand of bright yellow stranded cotton. Finish by adding small yellow glass beads in any available space around the French knots.

F l o w e r   B e d   5

W a r a t a h
See Diagram 5

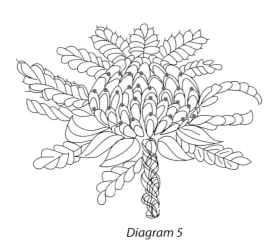

Diagram 5

Using brown DMC wool, work double whipped chain stitch for the stem. Starting at the base of

the flower, draw the outline of the flower's shape with a white marker pen. Following diagram 6 and using 4mm (¾₆") ribbon in two shades of red, embroider detached chains with a single wrap French knot holding stitch for each petal. Working in horizontal rows, gradually reduce the size and number of the stitches towards the tip of the flower. Add a few extra detached chains and French knots over the top of those already worked to give a three dimensional effect.

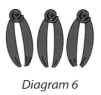

Diagram 6

Stitch the large red petals at the base of the flower, each with two long ribbon stitches side by side, keeping the tension slightly loose.

Embroider the three leaves to the top of the flower with fly stitches in medium blue/green 4mm (¾₆") ribbon and outline with small fly stitches to the top of each tip in a single strand of very pale blue/green stranded cotton.

Work the largest medium blue/green leaf to the left of the flower with pairs of straight stitches, the top tips outlined in fly stitch in a single strand of very pale blue/green stranded cotton and the central stem stitch vein worked in the same shade.

Complete with dark pine green 4mm (¾₆") ribbon leaves in straight stitch, some with single stitches, some as pairs.

Flower Bed 6

Summer Starflowers

See Diagram 7

Diagram 7

In four strands of very pale blue/green stranded cotton, work the three main stems using stem stitch.

Stitch the whole flowers each with five petals, the partial flowers with three petals. Following diagram 8, work in pale lemon and lemon 4mm (³⁄₁₆") ribbon in ribbon stitch with the centres stitched in colonial knots using four strands of lemon silk thread. In a single strand of lemon silk, work pistil stitches with two wraps around the colonial knots.

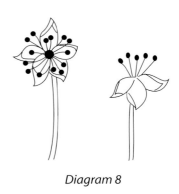

Diagram 8

Embroider detached chain buds in pale lemon 4mm (³⁄₁₆") ribbon. For the foliage on each bud, add fly stitches in a single strand of very pale blue/green stranded cotton. Add three straight stitches in the same shade above each bud.

Stitch the leaves in dark pine green 4mm (³⁄₁₆") ribbon, with the stitch pulled up tightly.

Heart of Flowers

T his project is suitable for both the beginner and the more experienced embroiderer.

It looks great framed or made up as a small cushion to display your favourite brooches or hat-pin collection. The design includes many different flowers and will provide plenty of experience for ongoing projects.

MATERIALS

Black, very dark green, plum or burgundy
    velvet 60cm x 30cm (24" x 12")

Fiberfill

Cord approximately 1.6 metres (63 ⅜") long.
    Medium thickness upholstery cord with a
    satin finish to match or contrast with the
    cushion fabric

Matching machine thread

1 metre (39") green 13mm (½") braid

Small piece of cream or tea-dyed antique lace

Embroidery ribbon 4mm (³/₁₆")

Three shades of pink – dusty, mid rose and pale

Very pale pink

Lolly pink

Burgundy

Pale green

Pale sage green

Dark blue/green

Dark green

Lavender – dark and light

Lemon

Cream

Pale blue

Embroidery ribbon 7mm (⁵/₁₆")

Purple

Pale pink

Blue/green

Cream

Mid olive green

Stranded cottons

Pale apple green

Mid blue/green

Dull green

Ivory

Ecru

Bright lemon

Needles

Chenille 20 or 22

Crewel for stranded cotton

STITCHES USED

Chain stitch

French knot

Ribbon stitch

Detached chain stitch

Fly stitch

Looped ribbon stitch

Stem stitch

Pistil stitch

Straight stitch

Colonial knot

See Diagram 1 on page 48.

Placement of the heart shaped template

See Diagram 2

Cut the velvet into two pieces each 30cm (12") square. Put aside one piece for the back of the cushion. Fold the front piece in half and tack along the fold line with contrasting thread. Fold again in the opposite direction and tack along the fold line. Trace the heart template (diagram 2) onto tracing paper and cut out. Fold the paper heart template into quarters and finger press along the lines. Match the folded lines on the template to those on the velvet and pin in place. Tack around the shape of the heart and then

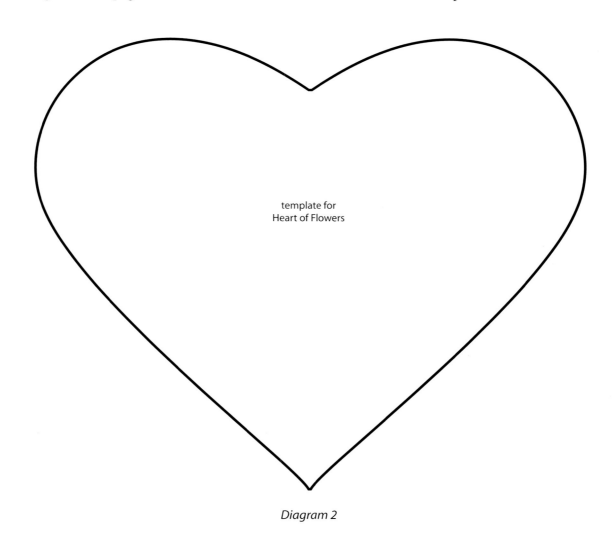

template for
Heart of Flowers

Diagram 2

Diagram 1

remove the pins and paper template. This tacking will provide a guide for the placement of the various flowers.

See diagram 3.

Start the embroidery at the top of the heart as indicated in diagram 3, working the design evenly around one side of the heart and then the other.

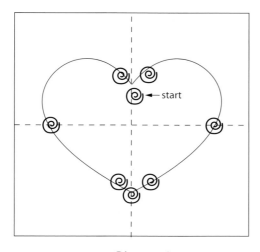

Diagram 3

Embroidery

Roses, buds and leaves

Stitch the top group of three roses and then the lower group of three roses.

See diagram 4

Diagram 4

The larger roses are worked in pale pink 4mm (³⁄₁₆") and pale pink 7mm (⁵⁄₁₆") ribbon. The smaller roses are embroidered in either dusty pink, mid rose pink or pale pink 4mm (³⁄₁₆") ribbon.

For the larger roses, starting at the centre of each flower, work three, 2 wrap French knots close together using 4mm (³⁄₁₆") ribbon. Change to 7mm (⁵⁄₁₆") ribbon and work two rows of chain stitch around the French knots, one row in a clockwise direction and the other anti clockwise.

Stitch the smaller roses in a similar way using only 4mm (³⁄₁₆") ribbon.

Using pale green and pale sage green 4mm (³⁄₁₆") and mid green 7mm (⁵⁄₁₆") ribbon, work the leaves in ribbon stitch, placing them around the roses.

Continuing around one side of the heart, embroider rose buds leading from the top group of roses in detached chain, the first bud worked in pale pink 7mm (⁵⁄₁₆") ribbon and the next two smaller buds in very pale pink 4mm (³⁄₁₆") ribbon. Add fly stitch foliage over each bud using a single strand of pale apple green stranded cotton. Place ribbon stitch leaves around the buds in pale sage green 4mm (³⁄₁₆") ribbon.

Delphiniums

Stitch a Delphinium, working three green buds at the top of the flower in single wrap French knots using pale sage green 4mm (³⁄₁₆") ribbon. Embroider the flowers in looped ribbon stitch using two shades of lavender 4mm (³⁄₁₆") ribbon. Add a straight stitch loop in a single strand of pale apple green cotton to the centre of each stitch.

Work three detached chain leaves at the base of each flower using dark green 4mm (³⁄₁₆") ribbon.

Daisies

Embroider ribbon stitch daisies in lemon or pale blue 4mm (³⁄₁₆") ribbon, each with three to five petals and colonial knot centers, in very dark green or burgundy 4mm (³⁄₁₆") ribbon. Place two daisies on each side of the heart underneath the delphinium and a partial daisy alongside the delphinium.

Single Rose

Using pale pink ribbon and referring to the instructions above, embroider a large rose and foliage under the daisies.

Single Daisy

Referring to the instructions above, embroider one blue daisy with a burgundy centre beneath the single rose.

Tulips

Following diagram 5a, work three stems, the two outer stems longer than the centre, in stem stitch using three strands of mid blue/green stranded cotton. Using cream, lemon or burgundy 4mm (³⁄₁₆") ribbon, embroider the flowers in ribbon stitch as shown in diagram 5b. Do not pull the petals to a point but leave a slightly rolled edge at the top of each stitch. Add a third stitch in the centre if there is a gap between the two worked stitches.

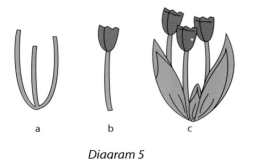

a   b   c

Diagram 5

Embroider the leaves in blue/green 7mm (⁵⁄₁₆") ribbon in ribbon stitch pulled firmly to a point. Finish with one smaller leaf using dark green 4mm (³⁄₁₆") ribbon as shown in diagram 5c.

Iris

Embroider two iris flowers close together. Using purple 7mm (⁵⁄₁₆") ribbon, work a single detached chain for the upper petal as shown in diagram 6. Stitch the lower petal in lemon 4mm (³⁄₁₆") ribbon, with a straight stitch passing behind the detached chain of the upper petal. Stitch a short straight stitch stem to each flower using 4 strands of dull green stranded cotton.

Diagram 6

Lilies

Work two lilies using cream 7mm (⁵⁄₁₆") ribbon. Embroider the petals in ribbon stitch and add the centre in 3–4 wrap pistil stitch using three strands of bright lemon stranded cotton. Stitch the leaves with ribbon stitch in dark green 4mm (³⁄₁₆") ribbon.

Going back to the top of the heart, repeat the embroidery down the remaining side.

Fuchsia

Stitch two fuchsia flowers and one bud in the centre of the heart. Start with the three stems in straight stitch using four strands of pale apple green stranded cotton.

Following diagram 7a, place two small straight stitches in pale green 4mm (³⁄₁₆") ribbon on each side of the stem, starting slightly above the base of the stem. Embroider the lower petals for the two flowers in lolly pink 4mm (³⁄₁₆") ribbon with three to four loose straight stitches, leaving space for the upper petals as shown in diagram 7b.

Stitch the upper petals in pale pink 7mm (⁵⁄₁₆") ribbon with three to four ribbon stitches as shown in diagram 7c, allowing the ribbon to loosen and twist a little.

To finish, work several straight stitches of similar lengths and one longer straight stitch in a single strand of ivory stranded cotton below the lolly pink stitches. Place a three wrap French knot at the end of each stitch in a single strand of ecru stranded cotton as shown in diagram 7d.

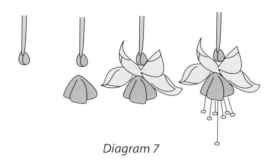

Diagram 7

For the fuchsia bud, place two small straight stitches using pale green 4mm (³⁄₁₆") ribbon on each side of the stem, starting slightly above the base of the stem. Embroider two straight stitches in pale pink 7mm (⁵⁄₁₆") ribbon. With a matching thread and approximately one third of the way down the pink straight stitches, stitch across the ribbon horizontally from behind the stitches, entering and leaving on the same spot as shown in diagram 8. Pull firmly, gathering the ribbon to form the shape of the bud.

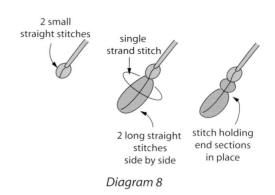

Diagram 8

Construction of the cushion

Carefully remove any tacking lines showing through the embroidery. Place the remaining velvet square and the embroidered front, right sides together and pin around the outer edge. Leaving a space of about 10cm (4"), machine stitch 1cm (³⁄₈") in from the edges with matching thread, rounding the corners slightly as shown in diagram 9. Trim the corners and turn through to the right side.

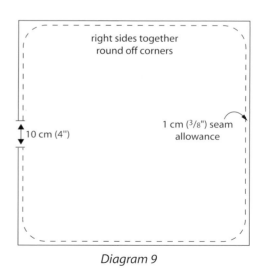

Diagram 9

Fill the cushion firmly with fiberfill and partially slip stitch the opening closed, leaving a small gap for insertion of the cord.

Tape both ends of the piece of cord to stop any fraying.

Insert approximately 40mm (1 ½") of the cord into the opening in the cushion and pin to hold in place. Place the cord along the cushion seam and on reaching the first corner, tie a knot as shown in diagram 10. Pin in place. Continue pining the cord around the cushion, making a knot at each corner, back to the opening of the cushion. Stitch the cord in place using double threaded matching machine thread, stitching through the cord and the cushion to hold in place.

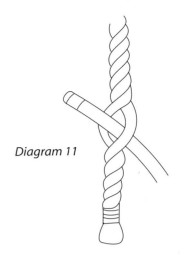

Diagram 11

Handstitch the braid and small sections of lace to the cushion. Using matching machine thread and tiny stitches, stitch the braid around the cushion alongside the cord and the lace across each corner as shown in diagram 12.

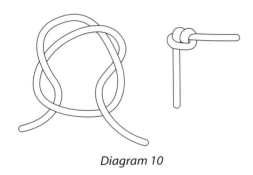

Diagram 10

Join the cord by pulling the end of the cord previously inserted into the opening out and separating the twists. Thread the just stitched end of the cord through the separated twist as shown in diagram 11. Trim any excess length of cord. Push the two ends of the cord into the opening. Slipstitch the opening closed.

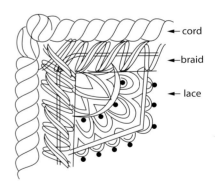

Diagram 12

Potted Wildflowers

This pot of Australian wildflowers is an ideal project to follow on with after stitching the Australian Wildflower Sampler. The same flowers are stitched with the addition of just three more flowers to balance the design and to add a little more variety to the range of colours. It is both a quick and easy project. The pot is cut from thin balsa wood and painted with acrylic paint. For a three dimensional effect, it is possible to embroider over the pot. Simply pierce the balsa wood with a needle, enabling the ribbon stitch leaves to trail over the edge of the pot.

Refer to diagram 5 for the template shape and page 116 for detailed instructions on making the pot.

MATERIALS

Dark green velveteen 48cm x 41cm (19" x 16")

Small piece of dark green felt 10cm (4") square

Chinese chop or Australian wildflower stamp

Thin balsa wood for the pot

Sharp craft knife to cut the balsa wood

Sand paper

Acrylic paint

Craft glue

Pale blue/green, red and yellow silk paint or food colouring

Threads

Mid brown perlé no. 3 cotton

Stranded cottons

Two shades of pale blue/green

Dark blue/green

Mid blue/green

Pale green

White

Ivory

Brown

Deep pink

Bright yellow

Red silk thread or stranded cotton

Brown silk thread or stranded cotton for the gum nuts

Mill Hill glass seed beads

Pale yellow

3 x 6mm (¼") beads for the gum nuts

Appleton 2ply crewel wool

Dull yellow

Small purchased bright yellow pom poms (if

not available, can be embroidered as Turkey knots using bright yellow embroidery wool)

Embroidery ribbon 4mm (3/16")
2 shades of bright red
Mid rose pink
Black
White
Very pale green
Dull olive green
Medium blue/green
Dark pine green

Embroidery ribbon 7mm (5/16")
Mid blue/green
Pale blue/green
Olive green
Lemon
Mid pink

Needles
Crewel 9 and 7
Chenille 20 or 22
Straw 3
Beading needle

STITCHES USED
Detached chain with French knot holding
    stitch
Detached chain
Ribbon stitch
Straight stitch
Bullion knot
Blanket stitch
Double whipped chain stitch

French knots
Fly stitch
Couching

See Diagram 1 on page 56.

Preparation

Make a paper template using diagram 5, then cut balsa wood following the measurements. Make the long cuts along the grain of the wood. Using fine sand paper, sand each edge to smoothen. Paint the pot with terracotta paint using downward strokes. Dry quickly with a hair dryer. Build up the layers of paint until you are happy with the colour. Paint white highlights on the left hand section and green/black shadows on the lower edges of the right hand section. Ensure that the pot is completely dry before handling. Coat the back of the pot with Aquadhere or similar adhesive and allow to dry. (This will provide better adhesion to the fabric when finally gluing in place.)

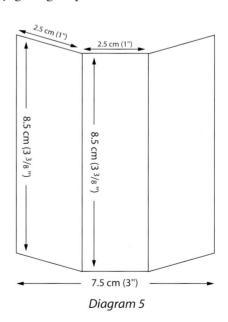

2.5 cm (1")   2.5 cm (1")

8.5 cm (3 3/8")   8.5 cm (3 3/8")

7.5 cm (3")

Diagram 5

Diagram 1

Centre the embroidery design on the piece of velveteen. Mark the position for the top of the pot using a white water soluble marker pen.

Waratah Flower

With a marker pen, draw a line for the stem, starting 4cm (1 ⅝") above the top of the pot and slightly to the right of the centre. Using mid brown perlé cotton, work double whipped chain stitch for the stem.

Embroider the waratah flower and leaves following the instructions in flower bed 5 of the Wildflower Sampler on page 43.

Sturt Desert Pea

Below the waratah, mark the centres for the three desert pea flowers, and stitch following the instructions in flower bed 3 of the Wildflower Sampler.

Using pale blue/green 7mm (⁵⁄₁₆") ribbon, add four or five ribbon stitch leaves in any available spaces.

Flannel Flower

With a white marker pen draw a small circle for the centre of the flannel flower and fill with 2–4 wrap French knots using 2 strands of two shades of pale blue/green stranded cotton.

Add the stem worked as a 10-16 wrap bullion knot using 3 strands of pale green stranded cotton.

For the petals, work eight pairs of ribbon stitches stitched side by side in white 4mm (³⁄₁₆") ribbon. Pull through to a point on the same spot for each petal.

On completion of the embroidery, paint the tip of each petal with very pale blue/green silk paint or very dilute green food colouring. Dry immediately with a hair dryer to prevent the paint spreading through the petals.

Wattle

To the right of the desert pea flowers, starting just above the top of the pot, embroider the stem of the wattle flowers using 4 strands of pale green stranded cotton, working in stem stitch for about 8cm (3 ⅛") in length.

Stitch the small wool buds in groups of 1–3 wrap French knots using dull yellow embroidery wool.

Add straight stitch leaves in medium blue/green 4mm (³⁄₁₆") ribbon.

If using purchased pom poms for the flowers, glue them in place at the end of the project. If using wool turkey knots they may be worked at this stage using bright yellow embroidery wool.

Long Ribbon Gum Leaf

To the left and above the flannel flowers work the gum leaf following the instructions for the leaves in flower bed 2 of the Wildflower Sampler.

Form the gum nuts following the instructions in the Wildflower Sampler and stitch in place.

Beaufortia Blossoms

Embroider ribbon stitch leaves using dark pine green 4mm (³⁄₁₆") ribbon and two blossoms above the gum nuts following the instructions for the flower tips in flower bed 4 in the Wildflower Sampler.

Heart Leaf Flame Pea Flowers

Mark the position for the centre of each of the three flowers.

ribbon stitch stitched through the side of the ribbon at the centre of the flower

Diagram 2

Using lemon 7mm (⁵⁄₁₆") ribbon, stitch the upper petals in ribbon stitch with two pairs for each side. Stitch through the sides of the ribbon towards the centre, leaving a slightly rolled edge as shown in diagram 2. Do not pull through to a point. Place a second ribbon stitch over the top of the first. Bring the needle to the front of the fabric at almost the same point as for the first stitch. Keeping the ribbon flat, enter the fabric again to the side of the ribbon, close to the centre of the flower, taking the needle and ribbon to the back of the fabric through the first ribbon stitch, tucking the stitch just under the rolled edge of the first stitch. Do not pull this stitch to a point, again leaving a slightly rolled edge. It may be necessary to couch the lower outer corners in place as illustrated in diagram 3.

the second ribbon stitch
placed over the top
of the first stitches,
couched in place
at the lower outer corners

Diagram 3

Below the four upper stitches, place two lower petals. Using mid pink 7mm (⁵⁄₁₆") ribbon, work ribbon stitch, stitching through the side of the ribbon towards the centre, keeping the ribbon flat and pulling to a point as illustrated in diagram 4.

the lower petals
worked as ribbon
stitches pulled through
the sides of the ribbons
at the centre of the flowers

Diagram 4

Colour the upper petals with silk paint or food colouring, mixing together red and yellow colouring with added water. Test the shade on a scrap of ribbon before using. Apply sparingly to the outer edges, building up the colour gradually, leaving the original yellow ribbon in the centre unpainted. Use a hair dryer to stop the paint spreading into any unwanted areas. Apply a little pink or diluted red paint to the lower petals and dry.

Embroider the surrounding olive green leaves in 7mm (⁵⁄₁₆") ribbon using ribbon stitch.

Pink Trailing Flowers

Work two 25–40 wrap bullion knot stems for the two pink flowers below the heart leaf flame pea flowers using four strands of stranded cotton. Thread two strands of brown and two strands of deep pink together in the needle.

Using dull olive green 4mm (³⁄₁₆") ribbon, work three ribbon stitches for the foliage at the base of the stems. Add a fly stitch at the tip of each ribbon stitch, in one strand of ivory stranded cotton.

Embroider the petals using mid rose pink 4mm (³⁄₁₆") ribbon in two to three long ribbon stitches.

On completion of the flowers, sparingly apply diluted red silk paint or food colouring to the petals and a very small amount to the green foliage.

Blanket Stitch Gum Leaves

Trace or draw the shape of four gum leaves with a ball point pen onto dark green felt and embroider in three strands of stranded cotton with blanket stitch. Work two dark blue/green leaves and two mid blue/green leaves. On completion carefully cut around the edge of each shape with very sharp scissors.

Leaves above the Pot

Using three strands of brown and three strands of deep pink stranded cotton threaded together in a needle, work a whipped stem stitch stem with slight curves just above the top of the pot.

Finishing

Glue the pot in place. Allow the glue to dry.

Add leaves to the worked stem in ribbon stitch using two shades of blue/green 7mm (⁵⁄₁₆") ribbon. Trail the leaves over the top of the pot, stitching carefully through the balsa wood to the back of the fabric.

Glue the embroidered blanket stitch leaves in place and pin to hold in place whilst the glue dries. If pom poms are to be used, glue in place.

Attach a Chinese chop or stamp with glue to the velveteen as shown in the photograph.

All in a Pot

This project is an enjoyable challenge for the embroiderer with some experience with wool and thread, but hasn't yet tried ribbon embroidery. Those with ribbon embroidery experience will also find this project satisfying. It is suitable for framing, or without the pot, is the right size to be stitched just above the pocket of a shirt.

The attractive pot used in this project can be made from salt dough, terracotta self-hardening clay such as Das or cut from thin balsa wood painted with acrylic paints. See diagram 8 for the pot template and pages 114 and 115 for full instructions on making pots.

MATERIALS

Green and white ticking 30cm x 35cm (12" x 13¾"). Furnishing weight fabric is the most suitable for this project. The design can also be stitched on plain background fabrics, velvet, damasks and checks.

Pot, pre-purchased, salt dough, clay or cut from thin balsa wood painted with acrylic paints.

Aquadhere or craft glue

Embroidery ribbon 4mm (³⁄₁₆")
Four shades of pink, from burgundy to pale shell pink
Dark burgundy
Cream
White
Pale lemon
Butter yellow
Gold

Lavender, dark and pale
Dark purple

Embroidery ribbon 7mm (⁵⁄₁₆")
Pale lemon
Cream
Mid blue/green
Dark blue/green
Olive green

Stranded cottons
Pale olive green
Dark olive green
Pale yellow/green
Mid green
Mid blue/green
Deep bright pink
Lemon
Gold

Needles

Chenille 20 or 22

Crewel 7 or 9

STITCHES USED

Stem stitch

Blanket stitch

Looped ribbon stitch

Ribbon stitch

French knot

Straight stitch

Fly stitch

Detached chain

See Diagram 1

Preparation

Fold the piece of background fabric in half lengthwise and widthwise and tack along the fold lines with contrasting machine thread. Mark the centre where the two lines cross with a water soluble pen. Measure down 2cm (¾") from the centre and mark the position for the placement of the pot as shown in diagram 2.

Following diagram 3, starting 1cm (⅜") above the marking for the top edge of the pot, embroider three main stems using three strands of mid green stranded cotton in stem stitch.

Diagram 1

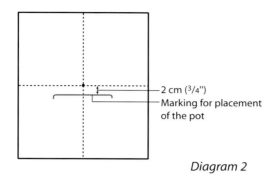

2 cm (³/₄")

Marking for placement
of the pot

Diagram 2

Starting at the base of the centre stem, stitch eight flowers in blanket stitch, using four different shades of pink 4mm (³/₁₆") ribbon, making each a slightly different shape, shade and size. Start with the larger flowers at the base of the stem, gradually reducing the size towards the top of the stem. Some may be partial flowers to fill in a space.

Add the centres of the flowers, each with a looped ribbon stitch in pale lemon 4mm (³/₁₆") ribbon with a straight stitch loop in the centre using two strands of gold stranded cotton.

Embroider pink buds in pale pink 4mm (³/₁₆") ribbon, with a single wrap French knot for each. Stitch the randomly placed green buds, each with a three wrap French knot in 2 strands of pale olive green stranded cotton.

Delphiniums
See Diagram 5

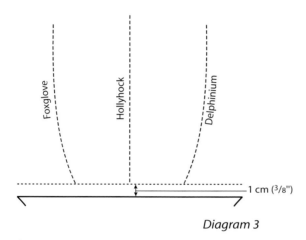

Foxglove   Hollyhock   Delphinium

1 cm (³/₈")

Diagram 3

Diagram 5

Hollyhock
See Diagram 4

Diagram 4

Starting at the base of the stem with cream 7mm (⁵/₁₆") ribbon, work looped ribbon stitch up the first third of the stem. Change to cream 4mm (³/₁₆") ribbon and continue with looped ribbon stitch until within 1cm (³/₈") of the top of the stem, gradually reducing the number of stitches.

Secure the centres of each stitch with a looped straight stitch using a single strand of dark olive green stranded cotton.

Stitch two buds in cream 4mm (³⁄₁₆") ribbon, each with a single wrap French knot. Using four strands of mid blue/green stranded cotton and with a three wrap French knot for each, add extra buds between the looped ribbon stitches to balance the spire and fill any spaces.

Stitch the leaves in dark blue/green 7mm (⁵⁄₁₆") ribbon in detached chain.

Foxglove
See Diagram 6

Diagram 6

Embroider the lemon foxglove using ribbon stitch, starting 1cm (³⁄₈") down from the top of the stem, in pale lemon 4mm (³⁄₁₆") ribbon for the first half of the stem. Do not pull these stitches or those stitched later on the stem to a point as for the leaves, but leave as a folded edge. For the lower half of the stem, change to pale lemon 7mm (⁵⁄₁₆") ribbon and continue to the base.

Add buds in three strands of mid blue/green stranded cotton with three wrap French knots.

Stitch the leaves in detached chain using dark blue/green 7mm (⁵⁄₁₆") ribbon.

Tulips
Embroider the four stems in straight stitch using six strands of mid blue/green stranded cotton.

Stitch two dark burgundy, one pale lemon and one cream flower. Work the petals with ribbon stitch using 4mm (³⁄₁₆") ribbon. Do not pull the stitches to a point but leave soft and plump. Add the leaves in ribbon stitch of varying lengths, using mid blue/green 4mm (³⁄₁₆") ribbon.

Agapanthus
Stitch four stems, each with a long straight stitch, using six strands of pale yellow/green stranded cotton.

Embroider two white and two pale lavender flower heads, working each in a circle of straight stitches using 4mm (³⁄₁₆") ribbon. Pull each stitch firmly to achieve the best tension.

Using mid blue/green 7mm (⁵⁄₁₆") ribbon, work the leaves with ribbon stitch. The number of leaves required will vary according to the space available.

Violets
Stitch the petals for the violet flowers in dark purple 4mm (³⁄₁₆") ribbon with two straight stitches for the top petals and three straight stitches below. Do not pull the stitches too tightly. Add a three wrap French knot for the centre of each, using three strands of lemon stranded cotton.

Embroider three stems just above each of the violets for the small purple buds in straight stitch, using four strands of pale olive green stranded cotton. Stitch the petals in straight stitch using dark lavender 4mm (³⁄₁₆") ribbon, with two to four stitches per bud.

Add foliage with straight stitch in four strands of pale olive green stranded cotton.

Yellow Trailing Flowers

Stitch four gold and two butter yellow flowers in straight stitch using 4mm (³⁄₁₆") ribbon as shown in diagram 7. Embroider two long straight stitches side by side, keeping the ribbon free of twists and pulled up firmly. Add four small straight stitches at the base of the two long straight stitches. In a single strand of deep bright pink stranded cotton, embroider a fly stitch over the tip of the four small straight stitches.

Work the foliage at the top of each flower in groups of straight stitches in three strands of mid blue/green stranded cotton.

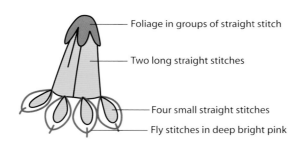

Foliage in groups of straight stitch

Two long straight stitches

Four small straight stitches

Fly stitches in deep bright pink

Diagram 7

Finishing

Using diagram 8 as a template, refer to page 114 for full instructions on making and painting the small pot. When the pot is completely dry, glue in place using Aquadhere or craft glue.

When the glue is dry, work looped ribbon stitches in olive green 7mm (⁵⁄₁₆") ribbon between the top edge of the pot and the embroidery to fill in any spaces not covered by the leaves already worked.

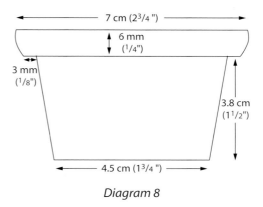

7 cm (2³⁄₄ ")

6 mm (¹⁄₄")

3 mm (¹⁄₈")

3.8 cm (1¹⁄₂")

4.5 cm (1³⁄₄ ")

Diagram 8

Ginger Jar and Chinese Lanterns

Ginger Jars have been popular decorator items over many generations and come in all shapes and sizes. Two designs, using simple but effective methods of colouring, have been included in this book. This design features the classic ginger jar and 'Anemone, Fuchsia and Ginger Jar' on page 100 features a larger blue and white jar.

In both projects the design is traced onto white fabric, outlined with fabric paint pens and coloured in with water colour pencils. The fabric paint pens have a brush like tip and produce wonderful colours. Both the pens and pencils are available from art supplies shops or large craft stores.

The coloured design is bonded to the background fabric before commencing the embroidery.

Do not be put off this design thinking you may not be good at painting. I have taught the techniques used in this project to many classes and the results have been quite wonderful. My students have been encouraged to go on to be quite inventive with their own designs.

As an alternative to hand colouring the jar it is possible to get a thermal transfer made at a copy or printing shop. Take the coloured design supplied in this book to the store for copying. The thermal transfer has a paper backing and is bonded to the white fabric with a very hot iron. It is then bonded to the background fabric in the same manner as the hand coloured jar. See Diagram 2.

I have embellished this project with braid, fabric and old buttons. Antique or old wares shops usually have a good collection of old buttons or look through your sewing cupboard for suitable bits and pieces.

MATERIALS

Background fabrics

Dark blue velveteen 30cm x 50cm (12" x 19 ¾")

Furnishing weight, jacquard fabric in dark blue and dull gold 25cm x 50cm (9 ¾" x 19 ¾")

White fabric 26cm x 23cm (9" x 10") This can be 100% cotton, 100% linen or a mixture of both, but should be of medium weight, with a close, even weave.

Decorative braids in matching colours of four different designs.

Twig with a curve.

Small scrap of sari type fabric (optional)

Five pearl buttons in different shapes and sizes

Dark green felt 23cm x 30cm (9" x 12")

Small amount of fiberfill

Matching machine thread

Embroidery ribbon 7mm (⁵⁄₁₆")

Dark olive green

Ivory

Hannah hand dyed silk ribbon 25mm (1")

Variegated greens

Wired ribbon 25mm (1")

Orange

Variegated orange

Yellow

Variegated green

Wired ribbon 32mm (1 ¼")

Orange

Variegated orange

Yellow

Variegated green

Embroidery threads

Perlé No.8 cotton

4 shades of green from dark to mid apple green

Perlé No.5 cotton

Pale blue/green

Marlitt stranded rayon

Apple green

Stranded cottons

Pale dull green

Very pale beige

Dark brown to match the twig

Silk paint or food colouring

Blue

Red

Yellow

Vliesofix for bonding the ginger jar and the braids to the background fabric.

Craft glue.

Watercolour pencils (choose from any of the following colours)

Aquarelle No.47 dark grey

Aquarelle No.4 bright yellow

Derwent 6 deep cadmium yellow

Derwent 2 lemon

Derwent 35 Prussian blue

Derwent 30 smalt blue

Faber Castell 409 deep yellow

Diagram 1 Template

Dark blue and deep yellow or gold fabric paint
  pens

Needles
Chenille 20 or 22 for ribbon work

Chenille 18 for 25mm (1") ribbon
Crewel 3 to 8 for perlé cotton
Sharp 10 to 12 for stitching the variegated
  ribbon
Straw 1 to 3 for bullion knots.

Diagram 2

STITCHES USED

Blanket stitch

Straight stitch

Ribbon stitch

Stem stitch

Bullion knot

Preparation

Machine stitch the two background fabrics together vertically to form one piece approximately 53cm x 50cm (21" x 19 ¾"). Press the seam edges together towards the jacquard fabric.

See Diagram 1 Template on page 69.

Transferring the Ginger Jar Pattern

Trace the outline of the jar and its design using tracing paper and a black marker pen (a laundry marker is ideal). Place the white fabric on top of the tracing and tape in place with masking tape. Using a light box or a window, trace around the outline and the design on the jar using a lead pencil.

Remove the tracing paper from the light box or window. Following diagram 2 (on page 70) and using a deep yellow or gold fabric pen, colour around the outline for the shape of the jar. Draw the lines at the base of the lid and the jar, firstly, in pencil then colour over with a dark blue fabric pen.

Starting at the top of the jar and using the blue pen, colour over the pencil lines of the design. Then fill in the blue shaded areas with watercolour pencils.

Using two shades of yellow watercolour pencils, colour in the background. Leave any area where the effect of light falling on the pot is required, white.

With a mid-grey watercolour pencil, colour the shaded areas on the opposite side to the white highlighted areas, particularly under the rim of the jar and at the base.

On completion of the colouring, with the iron on a hot setting, iron a piece of Vliesofix to the back of the now coloured fabric. Ensure the steam function is switched off.

When cool, carefully cut around the edges of the jar with sharp scissors. Peel off the paper backing. Place the jar so that one third is on the jacquard fabric and two thirds on the velveteen. Using a hot iron with no steam, bond the jar to the background fabric.

Select a curved twig and position it alongside the jar as shown in diagram 3.

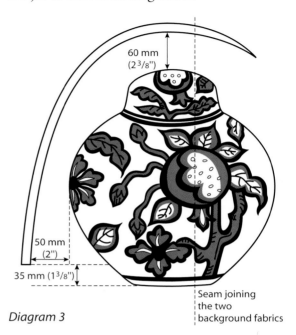

60 mm (2 3/8")

50 mm (2")

35 mm (1 3/8")

Seam joining the two background fabrics

Diagram 3

To attach the twig, using 6 strands of dark brown stranded cotton, couch with straight stitches about 2.5cm (1") apart along the length of the twig. Start at the end closest to the base of the jar.

Following diagram 4 and using a ball point pen, draw the outline for twelve leaves on the piece of dark green felt, varying the size and shape of each leaf.

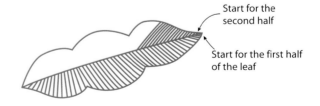

Start for the second half

Start for the first half of the leaf

Diagram 4

Embroider the leaves in blanket stitch, using four different shades of green perlé 8 thread and apple green Marlitt thread. On each leaf, any space showing between the two rows of blanket stitch may be filled with stem stitch using three strands of matching stranded cotton. This will give the impression of a central vein on the leaf.

On completion of the embroidery carefully cut out each leaf shape with very sharp scissors. Take care not to cut any of the stitches. These leaves are glued in place at the end of the project.

Following diagram 5, embroider approximately eight stems for the flowers trailing over the twig using straight stitch and pale blue/green perlé 5 cotton. Vary the length of each stem between 10mm – 25mm (¾" – 1").

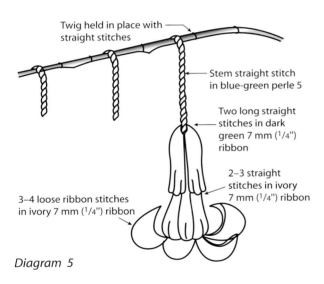

Twig held in place with straight stitches

Stem straight stitch in blue-green perle 5

Two long straight stitches in dark green 7 mm (¹/4") ribbon

2–3 straight stitches in ivory 7 mm (¹/4") ribbon

3–4 loose ribbon stitches in ivory 7 mm (¹/4") ribbon

Diagram 5

To work the flowers, stitch two straight stitches, one on each side of the lowest stem, in dark olive green 7mm (⁵/₁₆") ribbon using a 20 or 22 chenille needle. Keep these stitches free of any twists as shown in diagram 5a. Starting in the space between the two straight stitches, about 3mm (⅛") from the end, work two to three straight stitches using ivory 7mm (⁵/₁₆") ribbon.

These stitches should be pulled up firmly and be free of twists as shown in diagram 5b.

Continuing with the ivory ribbon, place the lower petals below the straight stitches using three to four ribbon stitches as shown in diagram 5c. To achieve a three-dimensional effect keep the stitches loose and allow to twist.

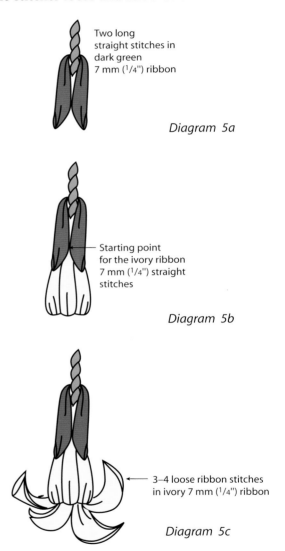

Two long straight stitches in dark green 7 mm (¹/4") ribbon

Diagram 5a

Starting point for the ivory ribbon 7 mm (¹/4") straight stitches

Diagram 5b

3–4 loose ribbon stitches in ivory 7 mm (¹/4") ribbon

Diagram 5c

Colouring

Mix together tiny amounts of yellow and red silk paint or food colouring and add water. Test the shade on a scrap of ribbon. Using a fine paint brush with a pointed tip, gradually build up colour on some of the lower petals. Use a hair dryer to quickly dry the paint between coats of colour. Leave some petals without colour on their lower petals and apply stronger colour on the tips of the upper petals. Sparingly apply a little of the same paint to some of the ivory straight stitches.

Colour the remaining ivory straight stitches with a dull green made by mixing blue and yellow together with water. Test the shade first and apply just below the green straight stitches.

Chinese Lanterns

See Diagram 6

Embroider seven Chinese Lantern pods following the instructions on pages 36 and 37 for the 'Autumn Sampler', garden bed 4, using 1m (39 ½") of the orange, yellow and green wired ribbon for each pod. Use the 25mm (1") ribbon for the small pods and the 32mm (1 ¼") ribbon for the larger pods.

Position each Chinese Lantern pod on the background fabric and pin in place. Insert a small amount of fiberfill stuffing under each pod to give fullness. Using double threaded invisible thread or a single strand of matching stranded cotton, slipstitch each pod in place.

On completion of the stitching add colour to

Diagram 6

73

the pods with silk paint or food colouring. Mix red and yellow to achieve a deep orange and deep gold. Paint the deep orange on to the orange pods and the deep gold to the yellow pods. Add the colours sparingly, drying with a hair dryer between each application.

Embroider the stems with long bullion knots in six strands of very pale beige and pale dull green stranded cotton. The number of wraps will vary with the length of stem required. Allow the stems to sit over the edge of an adjoining pod. Couch in place with matching thread.

Place the leaves along the stems according to the available space, some in variegated green 25mm (1") silk ribbon and some in dark green 7mm (5⁄16") ribbon. Use a size 18 chenille needle for the 25mm (1") ribbon and a chenille 20 or 22 needle for the 7mm (5⁄16") ribbon, with short lengths to avoid fraying.

Assembling the project

Cut two lengths of braid approximately 16cm (6 ¼") long, and two lengths of Vliesofix the same length and width as the braids. Iron the Vliesofix onto the wrong side of each braid. As the braids will touch the lower left side of the Ginger Jar, place the braid in position and trim the edges to match the shape of the curve of the jar where they will touch. Peel away the paper backing on the braid and carefully iron in place. Be careful when ironing the braids as some braids have a high synthetic content and may burn if the iron is too hot.

Arrange the leaves for the trailing flower in different positions before gluing, with some leaves above and below the twig, and others crossing over the top of the twig. Glue the leaves in place using craft glue or Aquadhere. Glue the buttons below the braids.

If using a small amount of sari fabric, secure in place with Vliesofix, taking care the iron is not too hot for the delicate fabric.

Refer to page 117 for instructions on how to frame this type of embroidery as it will require additional space created within the frame to accommodate the Chinese Lanterns.

Circle of Roses on a Wool Needlecase

This woolen needlecase is both beautiful and useful. It has pages to hold pins and needles and pockets to store a small pair of scissors, buttons, press studs and other sewing needs. The pockets face towards the centre of the case to prevent any items from slipping out. The embroidery design combines a range of stitches, threads and satin and rayon ribbons. Because of the different textures of the ribbon types, each of the roses differs in size and overall look.

MATERIALS

Navy wool blanketing 36cm x 20cm (14 ¼" x 7 ⅞")

Lining fabric 50cm (19 ¾")

2 x mid blue felt squares or ivory doctor's flannel 60cm x 16cm (23 ½" x 6 ¼")

Embroidery charms x 4 (optional)

Satin ribbon 4mm (³/₁₆")

Deep rose pink

Pale pink

Sage green

Mid blue

Pink — 52cm (20 ½") for ribbon ties

Rayon embroidery ribbon 7mm (⁵/₁₆")

Burgundy

Pale shell pink

Perlé cotton

No 5 pale green

No 8 olive green

Marlitt stranded rayon

Dark green

Very pale green

Mid blue/green

Needles

Chenille 18 for the satin ribbon

Chenille 22 for the rayon ribbon

Crewel 9 for the Marlitt thread

Crewel 3 for the perlé cotton

STITCHES USED

Coral stitch

Fly stitch leaves

Colonial knot

Detached chain stitch

Straight stitch

Ribbon stitch

French knot

Diagram 2

See Diagram 2.

The rose design shown in diagram 2 is repeated four times around the circle. It is sometimes difficult to get the four sections to look exactly the same and it may be necessary to add extra leaves or buds where there are available spaces to balance the design.

See Diagram 1

Diagram 1

Placement of the Design on the Fabric

Fold the navy wool blanketing in half lengthwise and widthwise and tack along the fold lines with contrasting machine thread.

See Diagram 3 Circle Template

Trace the circle template and cut out. Pin in place, matching the centre of the circle with the widthwise tacking line of the fabric, as shown in diagram 4. Tack around the outer edge with machine thread. Remove the template.

Diagram 4

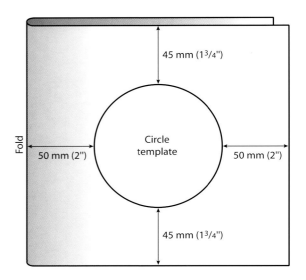

45 mm (1³/4")

Fold

50 mm (2")

Circle template

50 mm (2")

45 mm (1³/4")

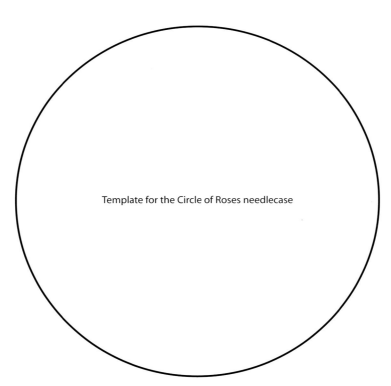

Template for the Circle of Roses needlecase

Diagram 3

See Diagram 5

Roses 3 and 3 in satin ribbon

Roses 1 and 4 in rayon ribbon

Diagram 5

Starting at the top of the circle, with a white water soluble marker pen, draw two small circles for roses 2 and 3 to be worked in deep rose pink and pale pink 4mm (³⁄₁₆") satin ribbon. Work each rose in two to three rounds of coral stitch, starting at the centre of each flower.

Embroider roses 1 and 4 in burgundy and pale shell pink 7mm (⁵⁄₁₆") rayon ribbon in the same manner, using a number 22 chenille needle. Using fly stitch, work a pale green leaf in perlé 5 and three olive green leaves in perlé 8.

Work three detached chain leaves using sage green satin 4mm (³⁄₁₆") ribbon and add several ribbon stitch leaves in the same ribbon to fill in any spaces.

Embroider buds in single strands of dark green, very pale green and mid blue/green Marlitt stranded rayon, stitching straight stitch stems with 2–3 wrap French knots.

Using mid blue 4mm (³⁄₁₆") satin ribbon, work the randomly placed colonial knots.

Repeat the design three more times around the circle working each section as evenly as possible. On completion, fill any spaces with small sage green 4mm (³⁄₁₆") satin ribbon leaves, buds or blue colonial knots.

Carefully remove the tacking threads showing through the embroidery.

Construction of the case

From the lining fabric cut the following;

- one piece to match the embroidered wool fabric
- one bias strip 35mm (1½") wide x 120cm (47 ¼") long. It may be necessary to join two strips together to achieve this length.
- two pieces 13cm x 20cm (5 ⅛" x 7 ⅞") for the two inside pockets.

Pockets

Fold one piece of pocket fabric in half with right sides together. Pin and machine stitch together 1cm (⅜") in from the edges. Leave a 5cm (2") opening to enable the fabric to be turned back to the right side. Trim across the corners and turn to the right side. Press the seams and slip stitch the opening closed. Repeat for the second pocket.

Pin the pockets in place on the lining as shown in diagram 6, leaving the edge of the pocket closest to the centre fold open. Machine stitch in place. On the left hand pocket, machine stitch a line of stitching 4cm (1 ¾") down from the top of the pocket to form two sections as shown in diagram 6.

Place the embroidered wool and the lining piece together with the wrong sides of both fabrics facing. Pin and machine stitch 1cm (⅜") in from the raw edges, rounding off all the corners. Trim off 5mm (⅜").

With the embroidered fabric facing you, pin the bias strip in place with right sides together and machine stitch all around, easing on the corners. On completion, clip the corners carefully.

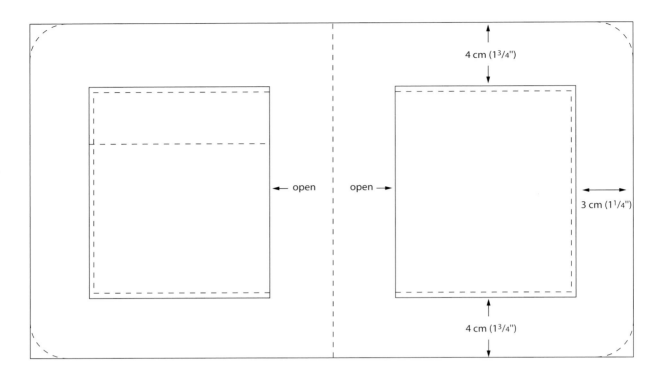

Diagram 6

Turn the bias edging to the inside of the case and pin in place. Cut the long piece of pink satin ribbon in half. Enclose one length in the middle of each of the shorter sides as fasteners to tie in a bow. Slipstitch the bias edging in place.

Cut the felt or doctor's flannel into two 30cm x 16cm (11 ¾" x 6 ¼") pieces and placing one on top of the other, machine stitch in place along the centre fold.

Make a small lining fabric loop and hand stitch in the centre of the needlecase to hold a marking pen. Attach charms to the front of the needlecase if desired.

Sweet Peas in a Blue and White Pot

This quick and easy project is ideal for framing and suits either an oval or round mount. The sweet pea petals are painted with silk paint or food colouring on completion of the embroidery.

The blue and white pot used in this project can be pre-purchased or made using white self-hardening clay such as Das, available at toy and craft supply stores. Alternatively, salt dough can be used. This will require several coats of white acrylic paint before the blue design is applied.

There are many and varied examples of blue and white china patterns. They are often found on dinnerware and ornamental pots and jars. It is worth trying out different designs to find one that you like and is easy to reproduce. After many trials the one I liked best for this project was found to be one of the easiest, but a little practice is required.

MATERIALS

Background fabric, black, dark green or dark navy velveteen 26cm x 30cm (10 ¼" x 12")

Pre-purchased or hand coloured pot made from salt dough or white self-hardening clay

Embroidery ribbon 4mm (³/₁₆")

Pale sage green

Dark blue/green

Pale rose pink

Burgundy

Pale lavender

Dark plum

Ivory

Embroidery ribbon 7mm (⁵/₁₆")

Medium blue/green

Pale lavender

Pale pink

Pale rose pink

Burgundy

Dark plum

Stranded cottons

Very pale green

Machine thread to gather the ribbon for the petals

Satay stick or tooth pick

Hairspray

Fine tip paint brush

Food colouring or silk paint
Pink
Red
Blue

Needles
Chenille 20 or 22
Sharps

STITCHES USED
Running stitch
Straight stitch
Ribbon stitch
Stem stitch

See Diagram 1.

Diagram 1

Preparation
Refer to pages 114–116 for full instructions on making pots and diagram 2 for the pot template. Once you have completed the pot and it is

completely dry, using a fine, dark blue marker pen, divide the pot's surface into small diamonds with straight lines as shown in diagram 3. Draw the outline of a cross in each full diamond and a partial cross in the partial diamonds.

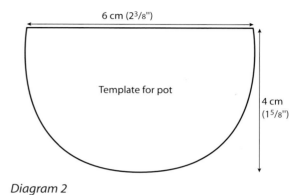

Diagram 2

Following diagram 3a, add lines around each cross to mark the area to be coloured in. Colour around each cross and add a dot in the centre as shown in diagram 3b. Complete with a dot in the centre of each of the diagonal lines at the point where they cross.

Diagram 3a

Diagram 3b

Fold the background fabric in half lengthwise and widthwise and tack along the folds with white machine thread. With small tacking stitches and following diagram 4, mark the position for the top of the pot 2cm (¾") down from the marked centre.

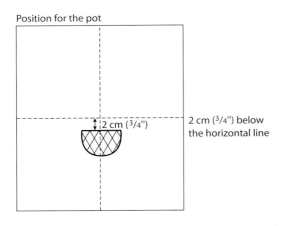

Diagram 4

The approximate number of flowers required for this design is 6 pale pink, 3 pale rose pink, 4 pale lavender, 2 burgundy and 1 dark plum. A few extra flowers may be needed to balance the design, as the size of each flower may vary. The main petals are worked in 7mm (⁵⁄₁₆") ribbon, each flower requiring an 8–10cm (3 ¼"–4") length of ribbon.

Sweet Pea Flowers

Using matching machine thread or a single strand of stranded cotton and a sharps needle and starting 1cm (⅜") from the cut end of the ribbon as shown in diagram 5, work very small running stitches along the ribbon until 1cm (⅜") from the end. Do not end off the thread.

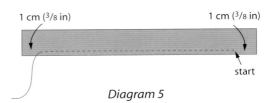

Diagram 5

Following diagram 6, pull up the gathers firmly. Cross over the two 1cm (⅜") ribbon ends and stitch through both. Fold the two stitched ends to the back of the gathers and stitch in place between the folds of the gathers. Trim carefully.

On completion of all the flowers, stitch in place on the background fabric using matching machine thread. You may wish to arrange all the flowers and pin in place before stitching. Stitch between the folds formed by the gathers, taking care not to flatten the ribbon by stitching too tightly.

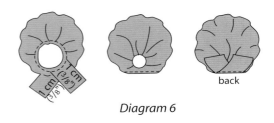

Diagram 6

Embroider the centre of each flower with two straight stitches, some in matching, some contrasting, 4mm (³⁄₁₆") ribbon as shown in diagram 7. Do not pull too tightly or twist the ribbon.

2 straight stitches
start side-by-side,
apart as they pass
to the back

Diagram 7

Fill the spaces between the flowers with ribbon stitch leaves using medium blue/green 7mm (⁵⁄₁₆") and pale sage green or dark blue/green 4mm (³⁄₁₆") ribbon.

Embroider three or more buds in any available spaces. Stitch the stems with three strands of very pale green stranded cotton using stem stitch. Following diagram 8, add foliage with pale sage green 4mm (³⁄₁₆") ribbon in ribbon stitch and the petals in straight stitch using pale rose pink 4mm (³⁄₁₆") ribbon.

Diagram 8

Some of the taller flowers will require stems. These may be worked as straight stitches in three strands of very pale green stranded cotton.

Form the tendrils using a single strand of very pale green stranded cotton. Wind the thread onto a satay stick, leaving a straight length at each end of about 8cm (3 ⅛"). Do not wind too tightly. Spray with hairspray until wet. Allow to completely dry before carefully removing from the stick, taking care not to stretch the coils.

Stitch in place using the straight thread left at each end of the coil. If necessary, hold in position by couching between the coils with matching thread.

Colouring

Colour the outer edges of the petals using pink, or red and blue together for purple shades with silk paint or food colouring applied with the fine tipped paint brush. Build the intensity of the colour gradually, drying with a hair dryer between coats.

Glue the prepared pot in place using Aquadhere or a strong craft glue. Remove any tacking stitches showing on the background fabric.

Pansies and Long Stem Roses

This project is suitable for framing and provides a good basis for further adventures into ribbon embroidery. It makes an ideal gift and doesn't take very long to complete. Only basic ribbon stitches are used, making the design suitable for beginners.

The pot may be pre-purchased or made with salt dough or a terracotta, self-hardening clay such as Das. All such pots may be painted with acrylic paint.

MATERIALS

Background fabric 36cm x 38cm (14" x 15").
    Checked cotton fabric in green/white, mid blue/white, yellow/white or mid blue/yellow is most suitable.
Water soluble marker pen
Pre-purchased, clay or salt dough pot
Aquadhere or clear drying craft glue

Embroidery ribbon 4mm (³/₁₆")

Lemon
Butter yellow
Gold
Pale green, two shades
Purple, three shades
Lavender, three shades
Pale pink
Burgundy

Embroidery ribbon 7mm (⁵/₁₆")

Blue/green
Olive green

Dark green
Plum for the bow

Stranded cottons

Dark purple
Perlé No. 8 cotton
Pale green
Perlé No. 5 cotton
White

Needles

Chenille 20 or 22
Crewel

STITCHES USED

Straight stitch
Colonial knot
Ribbon stitch
Detached chain stitch
Fly stitch
Looped ribbon stitch

See Diagram 1

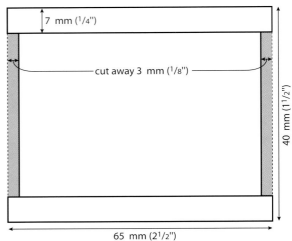

Diagram 2 Template for pot of pansies and long stem roses

Diagram 1

Preparation

Refer to pages 114–116 for full instructions on making pots and to diagram 2 for the pot template. Once the pot has been completed and the paint is completely dry, mark the position for the pot on the background fabric. Fold the fabric in half lengthwise and widthwise. Finger press along the two folds and mark the centre with a water soluble pen. From the centre, measure down the horizontal fold 2cm (¾") as shown in diagram 3.

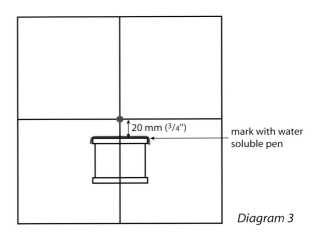

Diagram 3

Position the upper edge of the pot on a line of checks and mark with a water soluble pen. This mark will act as a guide line for positioning the embroidery.

The checks on the fabric help in positioning the first row of four flowers just above the top edge of the pot. Mark the centre for each of the flowers about 1cm (⅜") above the top edge of the pot with a water soluble pen.

Pansies

Embroider the petals for each of the pansies in straight stitch using three different shades of 4mm (³⁄₁₆") ribbon for each pansy. Refer to the photograph for colour combinations. Keep the ribbon free of twists. Work from the outer edge of each petal towards the centre, starting with the petals at the top of the flower as shown in diagram 4. The number of stitches required to form each petal may vary.

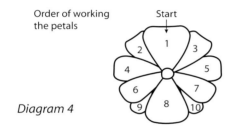

Diagram 4

Stitch pansy face markings on the side and lower petals with a single strand of dark purple stranded cotton, using straight stitches of varying lengths. Add the centres in lemon and gold 4mm (³⁄₁₆") ribbon, each with a colonial knot. Following diagram 5, stitch diagonal straight stitches in white perlé cotton in an inverted 'V' over the colonial knot.

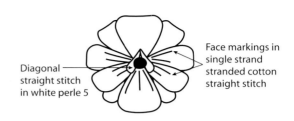

Diagram 5

Work the leaves around the pansies with ribbon stitch in blue/green, olive green and dark green 7mm (⁵⁄₁₆") ribbon.

Roses

Embroider the stems for the long stem roses in straight stitch with pale green perlé cotton, using the rows of vertical checks in the fabric as a guide for placement.

Stitch the roses in detached chain using burgundy and pale pink 4mm (³⁄₁₆") ribbon. Add fly stitches with some additional straight stitches in pale green perlé cotton. Work the leaves in ribbon stitch in two shades of pale green 4mm (³⁄₁₆") ribbon.

Wrap the plum 7mm (⁵⁄₁₆") ribbon around the pot and tie a bow. Stiffen with hair spray after tying, being careful to cover the pot with paper whilst spraying.

Glue the pot in place using craft glue or Aquadhere.

When the glue is completely dry, fill in any spaces below the row of four pansies and the top of the pot with looped ribbon stitch using dark green 7mm (⁵⁄₁₆") ribbon.

Cyclamen

The best time to embroider and colour any flower is when they are in full bloom. This is especially so for cyclamen. Having a flowering plant in front of you as you work is ideal, as you can observe the changes of light and colour on the petals and leaves. In this design, the flowers and stems are stitched directly onto the background fabric and the leaves are worked separately on felt and then attached to the background fabric. Colour is added to the flowers on completion of the embroidery.

MATERIALS

Background fabric 28cm x 25 cm (11" x 9 ¾"). This may be light or dark in colour with a plain colour or a hint of a pattern.

Dark green felt 23cm x 15cm (9" x 5 ⅞")

Dark green texta or fabric pen with a fine point

Small terracotta pot. This may be pre-purchased or made with salt dough or a self-hardening clay such as Das.

Acrylic paint, terracotta, white and green/black. (Optional, burnt orange or light red oxide paint)

Paint brush with a fine point

Red food colouring or silk paint

Aquadhere or craft glue

Embroidery ribbon 4mm (³/₁₆")

White

Dark green

Stranded cottons

Mid brown

Very pale green

Very light blue/green

Dark rose pink

Deep pink

Needles

Chenille 20 or 22 for 4mm (³/₁₆") ribbon

Chenille 18 for 4mm (³/₁₆") ribbon when two lengths are threaded together

Crewel needle for stranded cotton

STITCHES USED

Whipped stem stitch

Ribbon stitch

Straight stitch

Fly stitch

Blanket stitch

See Diagram 1.

Diagram 1

Preparation

Using diagram 2 as the template and following the instructions set out on pages 114–116, make a small pot for this design. Apply several coats of terracotta paint, drying between coats with a hair dryer. Be careful not to get the clay too wet. If a darker shade of pot is required, add a little burnt orange or light red oxide paint to the final coat. When completely dry, add white highlights to one side of the pot and very light green/black shadows across the base and on the opposite side. Set aside to dry.

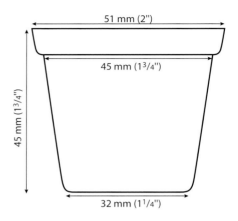

Diagram 2

Fold the fabric in half lengthwise and width-wise. Finger press and tack along the fold lines with contrasting machine thread as a guide for the placement of the embroidery and pot.

Measure 2cm (¾") down from the centre on the lengthwise fold and mark the width of the top of the prepared pot as shown in diagram 3. Use a water soluble marker pen if the fabric is light in colour and small tacking stitches in a contrasting thread if using a dark background.

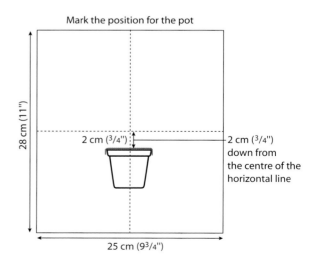

Diagram 3

Embroider the stems for the four full flowers in whipped stem stitch using three strands of mid brown and three strands of dark rose pink stranded cotton threaded together.

Some are full stems, other partial. Start the stems approximately 1 cm (⅜") above the top of the pot as shown in diagram 4. Stitch the stems for the buds in the same shades and stitch using two strands of each colour.

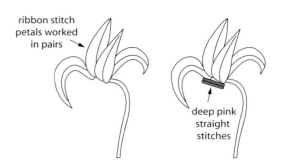

ribbon stitch petals worked in pairs

deep pink straight stitches

flowers 2, 3 and 4

flower 1 back view

3 dark green ribbon stitches

Diagram 5

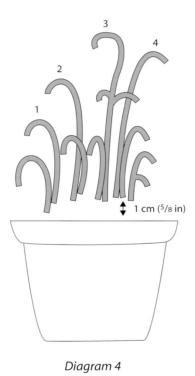

1 cm (5/8 in)

Diagram 4

Work the petals for the flowers on stems 2, 3 and 4 in white 4mm (³⁄₁₆") ribbon. Thread two equal lengths of ribbon together in a no. 18 chenille needle. Following diagram 5, embroider the petals in ribbon stitch, allowing the ribbons to twist. The number of stitches used in each flower will vary according to the effect required. I used approximately 4–5 pairs for each flower. At the base of the petals, work approximately four straight stitches using four strands of deep pink stranded cotton.

Stitch the petals for the flower on stem 1 in the similar manner as the others. As it is the back view of the flower, work three small dark green ribbon stitches below the petals instead of the bright pink straight stitches of the other flowers.

Following diagram 6, embroider the buds in white 4mm (³⁄₁₆") ribbon in long ribbon stitch using two to three stitches per bud, depending on the available space. Some stitches may require a little twist. Start these stitches from the top of the stem, placing them side- by-side. Enter the fabric at the base of bud almost, or on, the same point. Add three small ribbon stitches in dark green 4mm (³⁄₁₆") ribbon from the top of the stem on to the buds. Do not pull too tightly. Outline the tips with a small fly stitch in a single strand of very pale green stranded cotton.

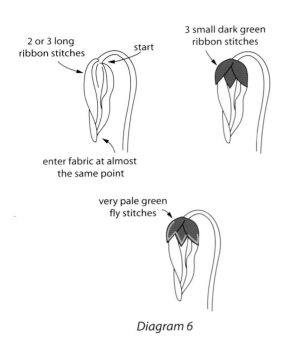

2 or 3 long
ribbon stitches

start

3 small dark green
ribbon stitches

enter fabric at almost
the same point

very pale green
fly stitches

Diagram 6

On completion of the stitching, carefully cut out each leaf with very sharp scissors, taking care not to cut any of the stitches.

Colouring

Add a little colour to the leaves with a dark green texta or a fine point fabric marker. Touch the thread very lightly with the pen as the colour will absorb quite rapidly. Try to leave a lighter edge on the outer edge of the leaves.

Colour the flower petals with a fine tipped paint brush using red food colouring or silk paint mixed with water. Build up the colour gradually, testing the colour before using on a scrap of ribbon. Dry between applications with a hair dryer. Leave the tips of the petals of both the flowers and buds white. Paint a little of the colour used on the petals to the top of the three green ribbon stitches close to where they join the stem.

Glue the painted pot in place on the line previously marked using Aquadhere or craft glue.

Arrange all the leaves in the available spaces and pin in place, allowing some to trail over the edge of the pot. Working one at a time, remove the pin and secure with a little glue.

Work twelve to thirteen leaves on dark green felt. Draw the outline for the shape of each leaf on the felt with a black ball point pen, varying the size of each leaf a little. Embroider each in two strands of very light blue/green stranded cotton using blanket stitch, working the stitches very close together as shown in diagram 7.

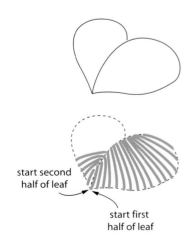

start second
half of leaf

start first
half of leaf

Diagram 7

Case for Glasses or Mobile Telephone

This simple project is perfect for gift giving or something nice and useful for you. It works equally well with different background colours and flowers. The darker background colours are more practical, but if necessary the case could be washed. The fabric used as lining should be pre-washed to avoid any shrinkage.

MATERIALS

Glasses case

Pure wool blanketing 11cm x 42 cm (4 ⅝" x 16 ½"). Navy, dark green, lemon and pale blue are all suitable for the purple, lemon and ivory pansies. For burgundy, lemon, rose pink and pale dusty pink pansies, the ideal background colours are navy, burgundy or pink.

Lining 11cm x 42 cm (4 ⅝" x 16 ½"). Checked, striped or small floral design fabric.

Matching machine thread

Narrow upholstery cord 69cm (27") in a matching or contrasting colour

Mobile phone case

Pure wool blanketing 11cm x 33 cm (4 ⅝" x 13")

Lining fabric 11cm x 33 cm (4 ⅝" x 13")

Navy machine thread

Narrow upholstery cord 63cm (25") in a matching or contrasting colour

Small press stud (optional)

Needles

Chenille number 20 or 22

Crewel for stranded cotton

Embroidery ribbon 4mm (³/₁₆")

Deep lavender

Pale lavender

Plum

Butter yellow

Lemon yellow

Ivory

Mid olive green

Mid brown

Stranded cottons

Dark purple

White

Pale green

Brown in two shades

Pale blue

Marlitt Stranded Rayon

Pale blue/green

Perlé 8 cotton
Pale green

STITCHES USED
Straight stitch
Whipped chain stitch
Detached chain
Colonial knot
French knot

See Diagram 1

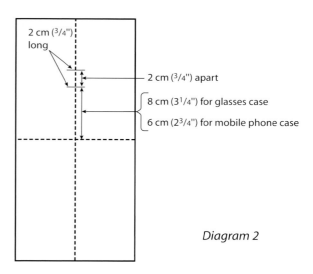

2 cm (³/₄") long

2 cm (³/₄") apart

8 cm (3¹/₄") for glasses case

6 cm (2³/₄") for mobile phone case

Diagram 2

Diagram 1

Preparation

Fold the wool in half lengthwise and widthwise and finger press the folds. Tack along the folds in contrasting machine thread.

From the centre, measure up 8cm (3 ¼") on the lengthwise fold line for the glasses case and 6cm (2 ⅜") for the mobile phone case and mark with a white marker pencil. Following diagram 2, draw two straight lines 2cm (¾") long and 2cm (¾") apart for the position of the base and the top of the basket.

Basket

Using six strands of the darker brown stranded cotton, stitch six straight stitches between the two marked lines for the wicker of the basket. Keep these stitches vertical and placed equally apart.

With mid brown 4mm (³⁄₁₆") ribbon, weave in and out between the straight stitch lines working approximately six rows of weaving. Keep the weaving as flat as possible and do not pull the ribbon too tightly. If the ribbon is slipping at the start and finish of each row, stitch in place using a single strand of matching brown cotton.

Outline the basket sides and base with four strands of the lighter shade of brown stranded cotton using whipped chain stitch.

Pansies

Embroider the centre pansy in straight stitch with the upper petals in deep lavender, the centre petals in pale lavender and the lower petals in ivory 4mm (³⁄₁₆") ribbon.

Embroider the side pansies with the upper petal in plum, the centre petals in butter yellow and the lower petals in lemon yellow 4mm (³⁄₁₆") ribbon.

Add a centre to each pansy with a two wrap French knot in two strands of pale green stranded cotton. Stitch the face markings in a single strand of dark purple stranded cotton with six to eight straight stitches.

Place two diagonal straight stitches in the shape of an inverted 'V' around the centre of each pansy using two strands of white stranded cotton.

Embroider the stems for the buds in straight stitch, using pale green perlé cotton.

Stitch the bud petals with one to two straight stitches using butter yellow or plum 4mm (³⁄₁₆") ribbon.

Add the foliage in straight stitch worked in two strands of pale green stranded cotton. Randomly place ribbon stitch leaves among the flowers using two shades of mid olive green 4mm (³⁄₁₆") ribbon.

Forget me not

Embroider approximately four small flowers, each with five petals and a centre knot. Some embroiderers find it easier to place the petals by working the centre knot first, others work the petals first and then place the knot in the centre of the worked petals. Work whichever method suits you best. Stitch the petals with three strands of pale blue stranded cotton in colonial knots and the centres with a colonial knot using three strands of pale green stranded cotton. Randomly place detached chain leaves using a single strand of pale blue/green Marlitt thread.

Basket handle

Using a white water soluble marker pen, draw the outline for the basket handle and stitch in whipped chain stitch using four strands of the same shade of brown as used for the basket's outline.

Construction

Place the right sides of the embroidered wool and lining fabric together and pin.

Following diagram 3, machine stitch the two fabrics together 1cm (⅜") in from the two fabric edges, rounding off the corners slightly and leaving an opening of about 7cm (3") for turning to the right side. Trim across the corners, turn and lightly press the seams only. Slipstitch the opening closed with matching machine thread.

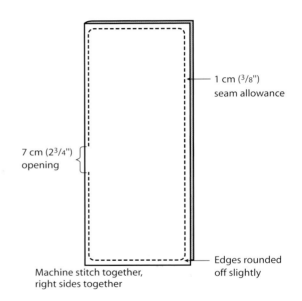

1 cm (3/8")
seam allowance

7 cm (2³/4")
opening

Machine stitch together,
right sides together

Edges rounded
off slightly

Diagram 3

Fold the case in half lengthwise with right sides together. Starting about 13mm (½") down from the top of the open end, slipstitch the two adjoining wool edges together down one side, leaving an opening 2cm (¾") above the fold for finishing the cord. Again starting at the open end, stitch down the other side, omitting the opening at the folded end. Turn to the right side.

Tape the two cut ends of the cord so that the cord doesn't untwist whilst handling.

Starting at the folded edge and leaving 3cm (1¼") of cord extending, following diagram 4, stitch the cord around the case. At the opening top edge attach the cord to the front only of the case and then stitch down the other side stopping at the opening left for the cord.

Take the extending 3cm (1¼") of cord, separate the twists and thread the other end of the cord through the space between the twists as shown in diagram 5. Pull together firmly and thread the two taped ends into the case. Stitch the opening closed and the cord in place at the same time.

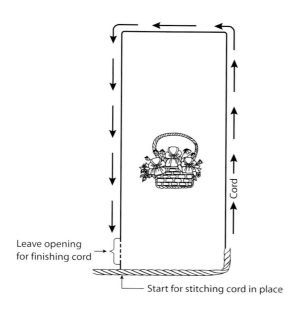

Diagram 4

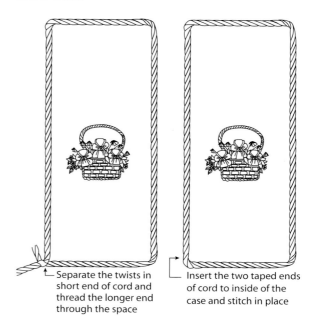

Diagram 5

If desired attach a press stud 2cm (¾") down from the top opening.

Anemone, Fuchsia and Ginger Jar

This project features an easy to draw and colour ginger jar. It can be hand coloured either blue or green, depending on your choice of background fabric. Most ceramic ginger jars are hand painted, with no two exactly the same. You should aim for the same effect and apply a little artistic license. I have provided instructions on drawing and painting the jar. The shape and design of the jar are traced onto white fabric, outlined with pigma pen and coloured with watercolour pencils. Several good brands of watercolour pencils are available at art supplies shops where they may be purchased individually or in sets. Some large toy stores and newsagents also stock sets.

A thermal transfer is also an alternative to tracing and colouring the fabric. Take the pattern supplied in diagram 2 to a copying and printing shop. The transfer is quite inexpensive to have done from the pattern copy. It can then be ironed onto white fabric and no colouring is required.

MATERIALS

Navy or dark green velveteen 60cm x 50cm (23 ¾" x 19 ¾")

Medium weight white fabric 30cm x 20cm (12" x 7 ¾") 100% cotton, 100% linen or a mixture of both

Vliesofix 30cm x 20cm (12" x 7 ¾")

Bright pink felt 23cm x 15cm (9" x 6")

Purple felt 23cm x 15cm (9" x 6")

Very small amount of black velveteen

Beads, approximately 150 very small plain black

Beads, approximately 250 small black lustre

Five dried lavender stems for the anemone (fresh stems can be dried in a microwave)

Small amount of craft wadding

Short length of string

Pigment textile pen, mid blue or green

Watercolour pencils, two shades of mid blue or green and grey. Suitable colours to choose from are

Blues

Faber Castell 445

Derwent smalt blue 30

Derwent Prussian blue 35

Greens
Faber Castell 467
Faber Castell 463
Derwent bottle green 43
Grey
Derwent gun metal 69

Sharp pencil

Embroidery ribbon 4mm (³/₁₆")
Two shades of blue/green

Embroidery ribbon 7mm (⁵/₁₆")
Mid blue/green
Olive green
Ivory
Plum
Lavender

Hannah silk 25mm (1")
Two shades of variegated green

Stranded cottons
Four shades of deep pink
Four shades of lavender/purple
Black
White
Dull blue/green
Mid brown

Silk threads
Dark pink
Ivory

Needles
Chenille 20 or 22 for ribbon.
Chenille 18 for the Hannah silk
Crewel for stranded cotton
Fine beading needle
Straw needle for bullion knots

Small amount of Aquadhere or craft glue
An interesting stamp, e.g. a postage stamp with
   a flower, a small square of fabric or lace or
   an old button
Food colouring or silk paint, green and red and
   blue to mix purple
Paint brush with fine tip

STITCHES USED
Bullion knot
Straight stitch
Ribbon stitch
French knot
Colonial knot

Preparation

See Diagram 1
If you are not using a thermal transfer or a design cut from fabric, following diagram 1 and using tracing paper and a dark marker pen, trace the main lines for the outline of the jar and pattern. Using a light box or window and a sharp pencil, trace the design onto the white fabric.

   To colour your pencil tracing, use a pigment pen textile marker with a brush tip and a smaller 'texta' type tip. This type of pen is available from art suppliers and larger craft stores. Use the brush tip for the bolder lines and the fine tip for the smaller lines.

Diagram 1

Use two shades of blue or green watercolour pencils for the areas of shading and background pale outlines of trees and leaves.

On completion of the colouring, iron Vliesofix to the back of the now coloured fabric, thermal transfer or fabric. Ensure that the iron is not on a steam setting. With the paper backing in place, carefully cut around the jar with sharp scissors. Remove the paper backing and following the measurements in diagram 3 iron in place on the background fabric.

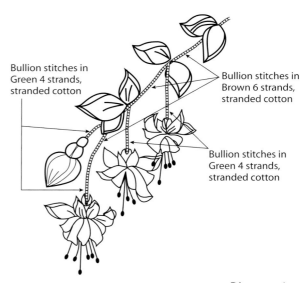

Diagram 4

Measurements for the placement of the jar

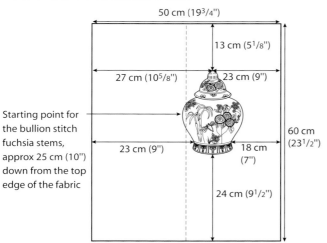

Diagram 3

Fuchsia

See Diagram 4

Stitch the larger stems in six strands of mid brown stranded cotton with 3 bullion knots using a straw needle. Work in three separate sections, starting with the one closest to the jar, about 25cm (10") down from the top edge of the background fabric. Each bullion knot will need between 45–60 wraps. Couch in place if necessary. The joins between the sections of the stems will be covered later by leaves.

Embroider three green stems for the flowers and one for the bud using four strands of dull blue/green stranded cotton, each in a bullion knot. Allow the two stems closest to the jar to trail over the brown bullion knots. These stems will require 15–45 wraps, depending on the length required or space available.

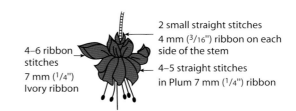

Diagram 4a

For each flower, following diagram 4a, , work two small straight stitches in light blue/green 4mm ($\frac{3}{16}$") ribbon on each side of the stem. Leaving a space of about 7mm ($\frac{5}{16}$") below these stitches, work the lower petals in 4–5 straight stitches using plum 7mm ($\frac{5}{16}$") ribbon. In the space left between the green stitches and the plum stitches, work four to six ribbon stitches using ivory 7mm (⁵⁄₁₆") ribbon, allowing some of the stitches to twist. Stitch several dark pink straight stitches of varying lengths below each flower using a single strand of silk thread and finish off each with a single wrap French knot. Add one longer straight stitch in a single strand of ivory silk thread with a two wrap French knot.

To stitch the bud, following diagram 5, embroider two small straight stitches, one on each side of the stem, in dull blue/green 4mm (³⁄₁₆") ribbon. Below the green stitches, work two slightly larger straight stitches in ivory 7mm (⁵⁄₁₆") ribbon. Do not pull the stitches too tightly.

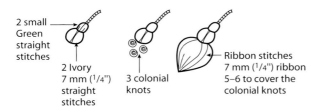

Diagram 5

About 3mm (⅛") below where the two ivory stitches finish, work 3 colonial knots using ivory 7mm (⁵⁄₁₆") ribbon. Starting immediately below the two ivory straight stitches, work five to six ribbon stitches side by side in ivory 7mm (⁵⁄₁₆") ribbon, over the top of the three colonial knots. Finish each stitch almost on the same spot to form the pointed base of the bud, keeping the stitches loose to give the bud fullness.

Embroider five leaves in two shades of Hannah variegated green 25mm (1") ribbon in straight stitch using a chenille needle. Place these leaves so as to cover the joins between the three sections of the brown bullion knot stems.

Add two olive green leaves in 7mm (⁵⁄₁₆") ribbon, each using two ribbon stitches worked side by side.

Colouring the Flowers and Bud

Dilute a very small amount of green food colouring or silk paint with water and apply to the tips of the ivory flower petals. Have a hair dryer ready to quickly dry the paint if it starts to run to areas where colour is not required.

Apply a little dilute purple to the bud just below the two ivory straight stitches. If using food colouring, attractive shades of purple can be mixed using red and blue. Only very small amounts are required.

Anemone

Cut one lavender stem in half. Wrap each of the four long and two short dried lavender stems or twigs with mid blue/green 7mm (⁵⁄₁₆") ribbon. Secure at each end with glue and tape in place whilst drying. These stems can be coloured with a little green paint or food colouring for extra effect.

When fully dry, remove the tape and tie the four long stems together with string and position on the background fabric. Stitch in place using two strands of matching stranded cotton.

To make the velveteen centres for the flowers, cut out two circles of black velveteen, each 30mm (1 ⅛") across. Stitch a circle of small gathering stitches 5mm (¼") in from the edge of the circle. Roll a small amount of fiberfill into a tight ball and place in the centre of each circle. Pull up the gathering stitches, tightly enclosing the fiberfill. End off the stitches and stitch down any excess fabric to the back.

Work fourteen to sixteen petals separately on

felt with 7–8 petals per flower. Following diagram 6, draw the outline for each petal on the felt using a ballpoint pen. Vary the size and shape of each slightly. Following diagram 7, embroider the main part of each petal in blanket stitch in three strands of stranded cotton. Use four shades of deep pink for the petals of the pink flower and four shades of purple for the petals of the purple flower. Using three strands of white stranded cotton, embroider straight stitches of differing lengths in the area below and some into, the blanket stitches.

Outline for the petals

Diagram 6

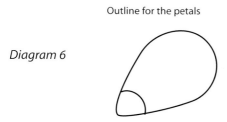

In a single strand of black stranded cotton, work randomly placed straight stitches varying the length of each stitch. Using a beading needle and black cotton, stitch the black and black lustre beads on each petal.

With matching thread, stitch the two shorter prepared lavender stems onto the background fabric, positioning them so that the ends closest to the flowers will fit under the petals when in place.

Arrange the petals before gluing them to determine the number to be used. Place the lighter petals at the top of the flower towards the jar, being sure to leave enough space for the black velveteen centres. Lap some of the purple petals over three of the long stems and, depending on available space, overlap one or two of the pink petals over a purple petal and one long stem.

When satisfied with the shape of the flowers, glue in place using a generous coating of Aquadhere or craft glue applied to the underside of each petal. It may be necessary to pin some petals in place whilst drying. Glue the black centres in place.

When the glue is dry, work the buds with 3–4 colonial knots for each bud, one in plum, the other in lavender 4mm (³⁄₁₆") ribbon. Cover with 5–6 loosely worked ribbon stitches in plum and lavender 7mm (³⁄₁₆") ribbon.

Loosely work the foliage around the flowers and buds in two shades of blue/green 4mm (³⁄₁₆") ribbon, allowing the ribbon stitches to twist.

Prepare the 'Anemone coronaria' label and string and add to the stems. If necessary, glue the corners in place. Add the stamp, button, fabric or lace and place between the jar and the fuchsia just above the pink flower.

It may be necessary to glue the knotted ends of the string in place before framing.

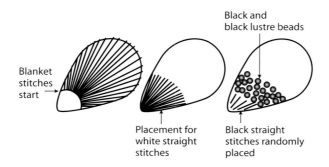

Black and black lustre beads

Blanket stitches start

Placement for white straight stitches

Black straight stitches randomly placed

Diagram 7

Navy Nightdress Case with Yellow, Blue and White Flowers

T his is a simple project designed to suit any level of embroidery skills. It would be a lovely gift for a special friend or relative, or for you to take when staying away from home for the night. The design can be easily adapted for many other projects where a corner design is required.

MATERIALS

Navy velveteen 40cm x 84cm (15 ¾" x 33")
Craft wadding 40cm x 84cm (15 ¾" x 33")
Lining fabric 40cm x 84cm (15 ¾" x 33")
Decorative braid 25cm x 95cm (1" x 37 ½")

Embroidery ribbon 4mm (³/₁₆")

Terracotta
Bright blue
Pale blue
Sage green
Pale lemon
Bright yellow
Mid grey/blue

Embroidery ribbon 7mm (⁵/₁₆")

Ivory
Bright yellow
Pale apple green

Stranded cottons

Pale apricot
Gold
Metallic gold

Marlitt stranded rayon

Pale blue/green
Very pale green

Needles

Chenille 20 or 22 for embroidery ribbon
Crewel for stranded cotton

STITCHES USED

Stem stitch
Detached chain with French knot
Ribbon stitch
Straight stitch
Fly stitch
Colonial knot
Pistil stitch
Detached chain

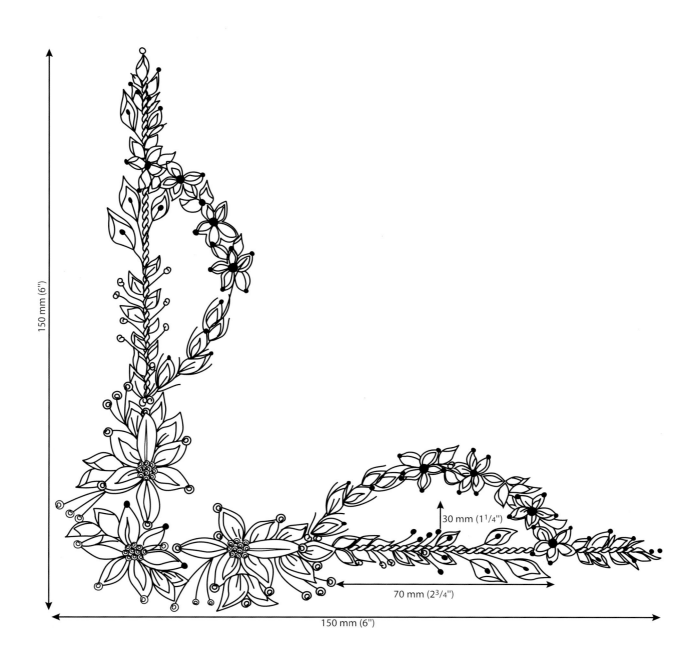

150 mm (6")

30 mm (1¹/₄")

70 mm (2³/₄")

150 mm (6")

Diagram 1

Preparation

See Diagram 1.

With a white marker pencil, draw two lines 15cm (6") long 7cm (2 ¾") in from the fabric edges in the lower left hand corner of the fabric as shown in diagram 2.

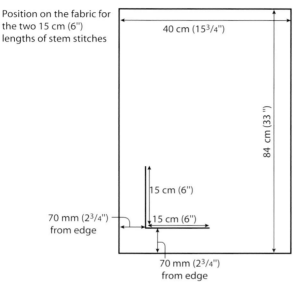

Position on the fabric for the two 15 cm (6") lengths of stem stitches

40 cm (15³/4")

84 cm (33 ")

15 cm (6")

15 cm (6")

70 mm (2³/4") from edge

70 mm (2³/4") from edge

Diagram 2

Embroider these two lines in four strands of very pale green Marlitt thread using stem stitch.

Following diagram 1, start with the large ivory daisy on the junction of the two lines of stitching. Work six petals using ivory 7mm (⁵⁄₁₆")

ribbon each in a detached chain with a single wrap French knot holding stitch as shown in diagram 3. Work colonial knots using bright yellow 4mm (³⁄₁₆") ribbon and colonial knots in two strands of metallic gold stranded thread, for the centre.

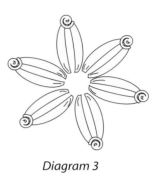

Diagram 3

Embroider one bright yellow daisy in 7mm (⁵⁄₁₆") ribbon on each side of the ivory flower in the same manner with the colonial knot centres stitched in pale lemon 4mm (³⁄₁₆") ribbon.

Using pale apple green 7mm (⁵⁄₁₆") ribbon, stitch ribbon stitch leaves around the three daisies.

Work four sets of three terracotta buds around the daisies in 4mm (³⁄₁₆") ribbon using colonial knots. Add stems in two strands of pale blue/green Marlitt thread with straight stitch.

Diagram 4

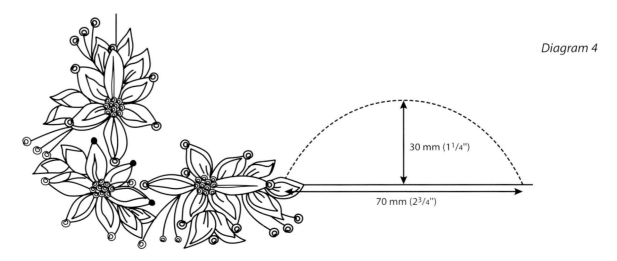

30 mm (1¹/4")

70 mm (2³/4")

Randomly place colonial knots around the three daisies using bright blue 4mm (³⁄₁₆") ribbon.

Following diagram 4, mark the position for the semi circles of blue buds and flowers with a white marker pen or tacking stitches in contrasting thread.

On one semi circle, work five detached chains in mid grey/blue 4mm (³⁄₁₆") ribbon. Embroider fly stitches around each of the detached chains using a single strand of pale blue/green Marlitt.

Using bright blue 4mm (³⁄₁₆") ribbon, work two detached chain flowers, each with 5–6 petals and a bright yellow 4mm (³⁄₁₆") ribbon colonial knot centre.

Add sage green 4mm (³⁄₁₆") ribbon stitch leaves. The number required will vary according to the available space.

Embroider two pale blue 4mm (³⁄₁₆") ribbon flowers each with 4–6 petals in detached chain. Add a bright yellow 4mm (³⁄₁₆") ribbon colonial knot centre and sage green 4mm (³⁄₁₆") ribbon stitch leaves.

Work the flowers and buds on the second semi circle in the same manner.

Working again on the main long stems beneath the semi circles, embroider leaves in varying lengths of ribbon stitch in sage green 4mm (³⁄₁₆") ribbon.

Randomly place colonial knot berries stitched using two strands of pale apricot stranded cotton. Add straight stitch stems using two strands of pale blue green and very pale green Marlitt thread.

Next embroider three to four lilies in ivory 7mm (⁵⁄₁₆") ribbon using ribbon stitch with pistil stitch centres in three strands of gold stranded cotton, each with three wraps. Repeat for the remaining long stem.

After the pale blue flower at the end of the semi circle of flowers, work one more ivory lily followed by four pale blue 4mm (³⁄₁₆") ribbon detached chains. Using a single strand of very pale green Marlitt, place fly stitches and detached chains around the blue stitches.

Randomly place colonial knots in bright blue 4mm (³⁄₁₆") ribbon in any available spaces between the leaves and the pale blue buds.

Construction of the Nightdress Case

Placing the right sides of the embroidered fabric and lining together, position the two fabrics on top of the craft wadding and pin round the outer edges through all three layers.

Machine stitch 1cm (⅝") in from the outer edges, leaving an opening of 15cm (6") to allow the fabric to be turned back to the right side. Trim across the corners and trim away any extra wadding on the seams. Turn through to the right side and lightly press the lining but do not press the embroidery. Slip stitch the opening closed using matching machine thread.

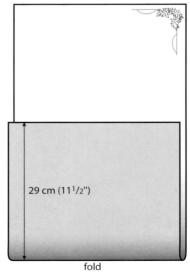

Slip stitch the two velveteen edges together with matching machine thread

29 cm (11¹⁄₂")

fold

Diagram 5

Following diagram 5, with the right sides of the velveteen together, measure and fold up one third from the unembroidered end of the fabric towards the embroidery end and pin.

Slipstitch the two velveteen edges together with matching machine thread.

Turn to the right side and pin the braid to the front third of the nightdress case following diagram 6. Handstitch the braid to the velveteen, using back stitch and matching machine thread. Attach a press fastener if required.

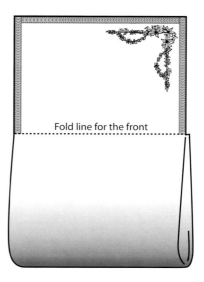

Fold line for the front

Diagram 6

Small Pots for Embroidery

Pots suitable for use with embroidery are available at craft stores. Obtaining just the right size and shape however, can often be difficult. I recommend making your own pots from self-hardening clay such as Das or from salt dough. Those made from salt dough take a very long time to dry but the resulting pot makes the effort worthwhile.

For larger pots, I recommend using balsa wood as it is very light. Balsa wood is sold in thin lengths that are easily cut to shape with a craft knife and is available at toy and hobby stores and some hardware shops. Care needs to be taken when cutting the wood that it does not split. With a little practice, very good results can be achieved.

Pre-purchased, clay, salt dough and balsa wood pots can all be painted to match the pot to the embroidery and to suit any décor. The terracotta clay pots look good left plain or painted as shown on page 60, 'All in a Pot'.

MATERIALS

Das self-hardening clay in terracotta or white or salt dough.

Small wooden rolling pin (available at toy shops)

Sand paper — medium grade

Plastic ruler

Small knife with a pointed tip

Acrylic paints and brushes

Aquadhere or similar clear drying craft glue

Salt Dough Recipe

1 cup (120ml) (4oz) of plain flour (all purpose flour)

½ cup (60ml) (2 oz) of salt

½ cup (60ml) (1½ tbsp) of water

Optional — approximately 1 teaspoon of wall paper paste, available usually in small packets at paint and hardware stores.

Mix all ingredients together and knead until smooth. Keep covered with plastic wrap to avoid drying out.

When using either self-hardening clay or salt dough, work with only enough clay or dough to make a single pot at a time. Wrap any clay or dough not in use in plastic food wrap to prevent it from drying out.

On a clean, dry surface, roll out the clay or dough with a small wooden rolling pin to a thickness of about 4–5mm (⅛"). A little flour may be required on the roller and the surface for the salt dough to prevent it from sticking.

For pots with rounded bases, use a small saucer or cup to trace a template. For the projects in this book refer to the design instructions for each template shape.

To make a traditional flowerpot shape, cut the long horizontal top and lower edges and the angular side edges with the edge of a plastic ruler. When forming a rounded edge, move the sharp knife around the shape to cut out the pot shape.

Make an indented line for the lip of the pot with the edge of the ruler about 6–7mm (¼") down from the top of the pot, taking care not to cut through the full thickness of the clay or dough.

Cut away the side indented portions as illustrated in diagram 1 with a sharp knife.

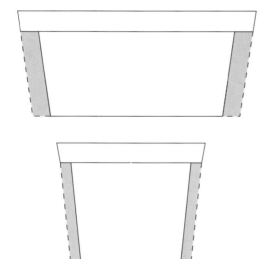

Diagram 1

At this stage the edges may not be absolutely smooth and can be sanded lightly as necessary

for the required shape. Sand the rest of the pot when it is completely dry.

Slowly dry the pot in a cool oven. This cannot be achieved in a microwave oven. For the Das clay, refer to the manufacturers instructions for the length of drying time required. Depending on the thickness of the pot, four to five hours of baking in a warm oven may be necessary with frequent turning. When using salt dough, even plain flour will rise a little if the oven is too hot and this will cause cracking. If you live in a very hot, dry, sunny climate the pots may be dried quite quickly in the sun with frequent turning.

Once the pot is completely dry, carefully sand as necessary.

For both salt dough and self-hardening clay pots, apply a coat of Aquadhere or similar craft glue to the back of the pot to seal the back and to provide for better adhesion when gluing the pot to the fabric.

The terracotta clay may be left unpainted or painted with acrylic paint for a more three dimensional effect.

Useful colours for painting either clay or dough are —

- Terracotta
- Light red oxide
- Burnt orange
- White
- Black
- Leaf green

Painting the Salt Dough Pots

Apply several coats of terracotta paint to the pot. Avoid getting the dough too wet. Allow the base coats to dry and then apply white highlights to one side of the pot and green/black shadows to the base and the opposite side. See Diagram 2. If a darker shade of pot is required add a little burnt orange or light red oxide paint.

Diagram 2

Balsa Pots

Balsa wood is an ideal material to make larger pots. Mark the required shape on the wood and cut into shape with a sharp craft knife. Longer cuts are made more easily along the grain of the wood, as thin balsa wood is inclined to split easily.

After cutting, lightly sand the edges. The pot can then be painted with acrylic paint.

Watercolour pots

The shape of a pot can also be drawn directly onto fabric using a black or brown fine permanent pigma pen. The pot can then be coloured with watercolour pencils. Care must be taken not to get the fabric too wet. A little practice before starting out will help if using watercolour pencils for the first time. Calico is an ideal background to practise on.

Acrylic paints can also be used for painting pots onto fabric.

Framing Your Completed Embroidery

MATERIALS

Frame. Non-reflective glass is not suitable for work where space is required between the glass and the embroidery.

Mount board. This is available at some framing shops ready cut to a standard size or can be cut to order. Large sheets of board in a variety of colours and bevel edge cutters are also available in art supplies shops.

Balsa wood lengths. Available at model making and toy stores and some hardware stores.

Backing board.

Crochet cotton and a large eye needle.

Glass cleaner.

Lint free cloth cotton gloves (optional)

Framing tape. Available at art supplies shops.

Hanging wire and eyelet hooks.

Framing your own embroidery with ready made frames can be relatively inexpensive and very worthwhile. Mount board can be added to the frame. This board is cut to size with a bevel edge cutter. This tool is quite expensive to buy, but if you intend to frame much of your embroidery and artwork, it will quickly pay for itself. Accurate use of a bevel edge cutter requires a little practice to begin with, but once mastered, is a very useful skill.

Good quality frames are also now readily available at framing and department stores.

Sometimes the colour may not be what you had in mind for your finished work but changing the mount and re-colouring a frame to your requirements is easy. Acrylic paint sold in small tubes is the best paint to use on the frame. With a little practice many different painted finishes are possible.

The raised, three dimensional nature of ribbon work poses a challenge when framing as space is needed between the background fabric and the glass. This is easily solved by using balsa wood lengths cut to size with a sharp knife and sanded for a tight, exact fit. These lengths are fitted to the ledge on which the glass sits, either between the mounts if two are being used or if only a single mount is to be used, it can be placed between the embroidery and the back of the mount. If no mount is to be used the balsa can be painted to match the embroidery or background fabric and set in place immediately behind the glass, thus creating a ledge for the laced embroidery to sit on.

Lacing embroidery for framing

Time spent lacing the embroidery to a backing board is well spent. Crochet cotton is ideal for the job, being strong, inexpensive and readily available.

Fold two opposite edges of the embroidered fabric inward over the cardboard, checking that the design is centred on the backing and that the fabric is smooth at the front. Using crochet cotton and a large eye needle, start lacing from the centre of one edge, taking the stitches from under the fabric across to the opposite side. Bring the needle out again to the front of the fold. Keep the stitches approximately 12mm (½") to 25mm (1") apart, depending on the amount of fabric available to fold under. Continue stitching in this manner until reaching the end of the backing cardboard and end off the thread securely.

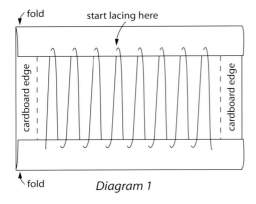

Diagram 1

Re-thread the needle and starting again in the centre of the same edge, stitch in the opposite direction, lacing the folds together and ending off firmly.

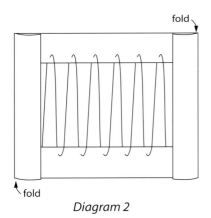

Diagram 2

Fold the remaining fabric edges neatly inward checking that the design remains centred and the front smooth.

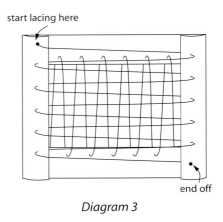

Diagram 3

Starting in the left hand corner and following the instructions described for sides 1 and 2, lace across to the right hand side and end off firmly.

It is very important to thoroughly clean the glass used for the frame. Try to clean the glass in daylight, as at night, even after cleaning, marks on the glass are not always obvious. A pair of cotton gloves for holding the glass whilst cleaning is a help, as is a lint free cloth.

To secure the back of the frame it is best to use special framing tape as it is strong and long lasting. Sometimes it is tempting to use packing or masking tape but these do not last as well in very hot or humid climates.

Picture hanging wire and eyelet hooks are readily available at hardware stores to finish off the job.

Glossary of Stitches

Threading the needle for ribbon embroidery

Blanket stitch

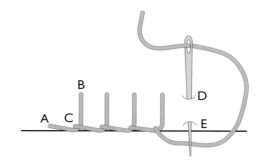

Cut the embroidery ribbon at an angle and thread through the eye of a chenille needle.

Insert the point of the needle through the centre of the ribbon, about 7mm (¼") from the end.

With the long end of the ribbon, pull the ribbon firmly until the ribbon knots on the needle's eye.

Work with short lengths of ribbon about 30cm (12") long to avoid tangling and wear and tear on the ribbon, particularly silk ribbon. Rayon ribbon is a little less prone to wear and tear and more suited to embroidery on articles to be worn and washed.

A knot can be used when starting ribbon embroidery. It is also possible to leave a 2.5cm (1") tail as an alternative method of starting off. On completion of the embroidery the tails should be stitched to the centre of the work, particularly if using fine fabrics.

This useful stitch is popular for appliqué and as a traditional edge for blankets.

Bring the thread to the right side of the fabric at point A. Take the needle and thread to the back of the fabric at point B. Re-enter the fabric at point C with the thread under the needle.

Pull the thread so that the stitch sits on the edge of the fabric.

Take the needle to the back of the fabric at point D and re-emerge on the front of the fabric at point E.

Continue to work with evenly spaced stitches.

Blanket stitch worked in a circle

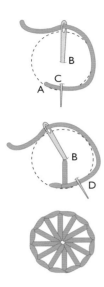

Worked in thread, wool or ribbon, blanket stitch embroidered in a circle is ideal for hollyhock flowers. The circle shape for the centre of the flower may be drawn onto the fabric with a white marker pencil for dark fabric or a blue water soluble pen for lighter colours.

Bring the needle to the right side of the fabric at A. Take the needle from B to C. With the thread under the tip of the needle, pull the thread through so that the loop sits on the edge of the circle.

Continue working evenly around the circle, turning the fabric as the stitches are worked.

On completion, take the needle from the centre to A with the thread under the needle. Pull through to the back of the fabric and end off.

Bullion Knot

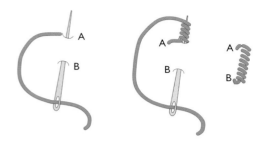

Bring the needle and thread to the front of the fabric at A.

Take the needle to the back of the fabric at B and re-enter the fabric to the front at A.

Wrap the thread around the needle, the number of wraps varying according to the length of the bullion stitch required.

Ease the needle through the wraps and fabric, keeping a thumb on top of the wraps whilst pulling through to maintain an even tension on the wraps. Pull the thread all the way through and ensure all the wraps are firm and even.

Take the needle to the back of the fabric at B to anchor the knot. Pull thread through and end off.

Chain stitch

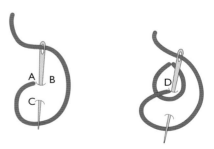

Bring the needle to the front at A. Take the needle to the back of the fabric at B without going through the same hole. Re-enter the fabric at C keeping the tip of the needle over the thread loop.

Pull the thread through to form the first chain stitch.

To make the next chain stitch, re-enter the first chain at D and repeat steps1 and 2.

Colonial knot

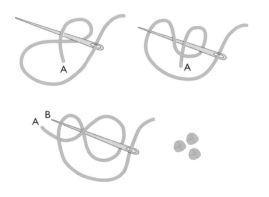

Used often for candlewicking, the colonial knot is more uniform in size and shape than the French knot when several are worked in the same thread and number of strands. It is a firmer knot that works equally well in thread, wool or ribbon.

Bring the needle to the front at A and place the needle under the thread.

Bring the thread up towards the point of the needle.

Place the thread under the point of the needle to form a figure of eight with the thread.

Re-enter the fabric at B, about one needle width away from point A, keeping the needle vertical whilst tightening the thread firmly around the needle. Hold the knot in place whilst pulling the needle through the fabric.

Coral stitch

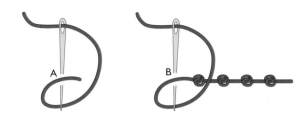

Coral stitch is a useful stitch for forming an outline and is often used in crewel embroidery. It is usually worked on a straight line or a curve, but can also be worked in a fairly tight circle in various types of thread or embroidery ribbon.

When stitched in stranded or perlé cotton worked in a circle, coral stitch can produce attractive full roses or when worked in wool, agapanthus heads. If worked in embroidery ribbon in a circle, it is necessary to keep the ribbon flat and free of twists for the best effect.

Bring the needle and thread to the front of the fabric, take a small bite of the fabric at A, taking the thread over the top of the needle and under the tip of the needle and pull through.

Move on to point B and repeat.

Couching

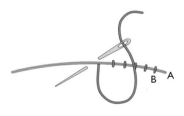

Couching may be used to provide an outline or as a method of holding a thread, ribbon or very long bullion stitch in a particular shape or form.

Bring the thread to be held in place to the

front of the fabric at A. Lay on the fabric in the desired direction. Bring the couching thread to the front just above the laid thread. Take the couching thread to the back of the fabric at B over the laid thread.

Pull the thread through to form a very short straight stitch. Re-enter the fabric a short distance along the laid thread and repeat the above steps to hold the thread in place.

Complete the couching stitches and end off both threads at the back of the fabric.

Detached Chain (Lazy Daisy Stitch)

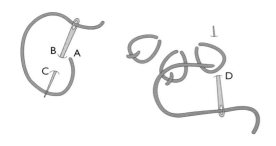

Bring the needle to the front at A. Without going through the same hole, take the needle and thread to the back of the fabric at B. Re-enter at the front of the fabric at C, taking the tip of the needle over the loop of thread that has formed.

Go to the back of the fabric at D to form a holding stitch.

Fly Stitch

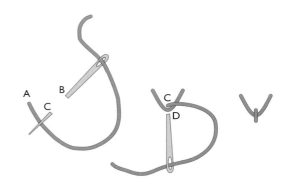

Bring the needle and thread to the front of the fabric at A.

Take the needle to the back of the fabric at B. Re-enter the fabric at C with the loop of thread under the needle.

Pull the needle and thread through until the looped thread lies flat against the fabric.

Take the thread to the back of the fabric at D to anchor the loop. Finish off the thread.

Fly Stitch Leaves

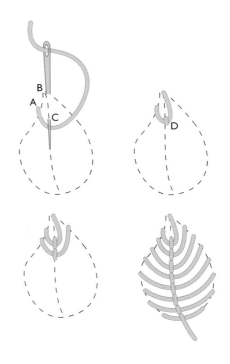

Draw the outline shape of the leaf and central vein.

Leaf curling to the left

Bring the needle and thread to the right side of the fabric entering at A on the left of the leaf, slightly below its tip.

Take the needle and thread to the back of the work on the tip of the leaf at B on the central vein. Re-enter at C, keeping the thread under the needle.

Pull the thread through and anchor the thread loop by taking the needle and thread to the back of the fabric at D.

Work a second fly stitch below the first. To ensure the leaf curls to the left, keep the left side stitches shorter than the right.

Work more fly stitches in the same manner to fill the leaf shape, finishing off the last fly stitch with a longer holding stitch.

For a leaf curling to the right, reverse the directions.

French knot

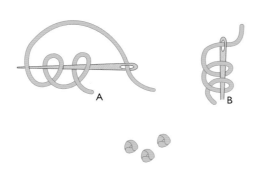

Bring the needle and thread to the front of the fabric at A. Wrap the thread around the needle, the number of wraps will depend on the size of the knot required.

Re-enter the fabric at B, which should be about a needle width away from A.

Pull the thread through to the back of the fabric to secure and finish off.

Pistil stitch

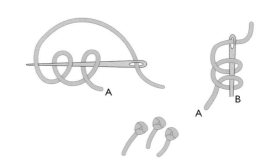

Enter the fabric at A. Twist the thread around the needle as for a French knot.

Re-enter the fabric at B, pull the thread to the back of the work and finish off.

Ribbon stitch

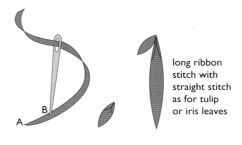

long ribbon stitch with straight stitch as for tulip or iris leaves

This stitch is used for both petals and leaves. It can be worked with the ribbon flat against the background fabric, as in daisy petals or slightly looped whilst inserting the needle through the ribbon and fabric for a more three dimensional effect for the leaves.

Bring the needle and ribbon to the front of the fabric at A and flatten the ribbon on the fabric. Insert the needle at B and carefully pull through to the back of the fabric to form a point towards the tip of the stitch. Do not pull too tightly. If a tip pointing sideways is required the needle may be inserted at the side of the ribbon in which direction the tip is to point and pulled through as above.

Looped ribbon stitch

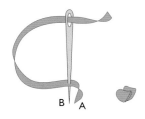

This stitch is ideal for the individual petals of the delphinium and for the raised centres of other flowers.

Bring the needle and ribbon to the front of the fabric at A. Make a small loop in the ribbon, insert the needle through the centre of the ribbon and re-enter the fabric at B, close to A but not the same hole.

Gently pull through and leave a second small ribbon loop. Finish off at the back.

If this stitch is to be used for a small petal, a single strand straight stitch loop in contrasting cotton may be placed in the centre to secure.

Stem stitch

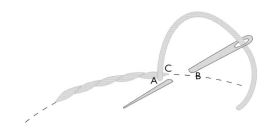

With a water soluble marker pen, draw a guideline for the placement of the line of stitching.

Working from left to right with the thread below the needle, bring the needle up through the fabric at A. Go back down into the fabric at B, come out again at C, which should be halfway along the length of the previous stitch.

Continue along the length of line to be stitched and finish off the thread.

Whipped stem stitch

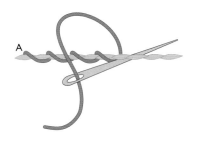

Work the required length of stem stitch.

To whip, bring the needle to the front of the fabric at A, take the thread over the top of the stem stitch and back under the next.

Continue taking the thread over and under the first row of stem stitches.

These stitches may be double whipped for a more rounded, bolder look, by stitching two rows whipped stitches, starting one from each side of the row of stem stitch.

Turkey Stitch or Ghiordes Knot

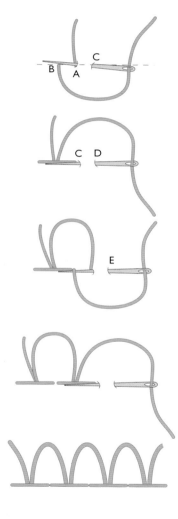

This stitch may be successfully worked in stranded cotton, perlé cotton and best of all in wool. When the loops are cut and combed or brushed out, tuffs are formed. Each stitch may be worked individually or in groups. A small tooth brush is ideal for brushing the cut loops.

At A, take the needle and thread to the back of the fabric, pull the thread through leaving a long tail of thread at the front. Re-enter the fabric at B, a short distance from A.

Pull the thread through gently, with the thread below the needle. Take the needle to the back of the fabric at C. Pull the thread to the back of the fabric, to form the first backstitch. Bring the needle to the front of the fabric at A. Pull the thread through to the front of the fabric with the thread above. Take the needle to the back of the fabric at D to form the first loop. Holding the loop and the tail flat on the fabric under the thumb, bring the needle to the front of the fabric at C. Keeping the thread below, take the needle to the back of the fabric at E. This forms the second backstitch. Continue until the required number of loops are worked, ending with the final stitch as a back stitch, leaving a tail of thread at the front of the fabric.

Trim and cut all the loops, smooth the loops and gently brush to fluff out.

Whipped chain stitch

Work a row of chain stitch to the required length. Thread a second thread and whip at even intervals using a blunt ended tapestry needle.

Bring the needle and thread to the front of the fabric. Pass the thread over the top and behind each chain stitch, from left to right, without picking up the background fabric.

To double whip chain stitch for use as a bolder stitch, work the second whipped stitch over the first in the opposite direction from right to left.

Detached Chain with a French Knot Holding Stitch

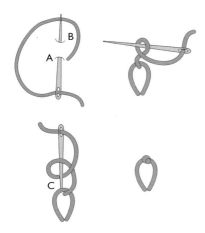

I have used this stitch for the petals of the Waratah in the Australian Wildflower Sampler and for the large ivory daisies in the Navy Nightdress Case with Yellow, Blue and White Flowers.

Bring the needle to the front of the fabric at A. Re-enter the fabric alongside A. Take the needle to the back of the fabric, re-emerging at B, keeping the thread below the needle.

Pull the thread through to form a detached chain loop and twist the thread round the needle as for a French knot. Re-enter the fabric at C to form a holding stitch.

SUPPLIERS DETAILS

Supplier of Mokuba and rayon
embroidery ribbons

DESIGNER TRIM PTY LTD
387 BRIDGE ROAD
RICHMOND
VICTORIA 3121
AUSTRALIA
PH 61 3 94284897
FAX 61 3 94292702

Supplier of Hannah embroidery ribbons

RISTAL THREADS
PO BOX 134
MITCHEL
ACT 2911
AUSTRALIA
PH 61 2 62412293
WWW.RISTALTHREADS.COM
INFO@RISTALTHREADS.COM

Supplier of Sillook rayon embroidery ribbons

AGENCY ONE
85A PAYNEHAM ROAD
ST PETERS
SOUTH AUSTRALIA 5069
PH 61 8 83631800
FAX 61 8 83631951
WWW.AGENCYONE@OZEMAIL.COM.AU

Supplier of satin embroidery ribbons, fabrics,
upholstery braids and cords, Madiera stranded
cottons and silks

SIMPLY FABRICS
260 MAGILL ROAD
BEULAH PARK
SOUTH AUSTRALIA 5067
PH 61 8 83640064

Supplier of D.M.C. stranded cottons

RADDA AUSTRALIA
PH 61 2 95593088
FAX 61 2 95595338
TOLL FREE (within Australia)
PH 1800 684144
TOLL FREE (within Australia)
FAX 1800 684244

Supplier of Rajhamal art silk thread

RAJMAHAL art. silk
PH 61 3 54417787
FAX 61 3 54417959

Supplier of Anchor stranded cottons,
Appleton and Paterna wools and upholstery
fabrics and cords

LINCRAFT
MYER CENTRE
RUNDLE MALL
ADELAIDE 5000
AUSTRALIA
PH 61 8 82316611

Supplier of frames, framing supplies, mounts,
cutters and tape

PREMIER ART SUPPLIES PTY LTD
43 GILLIES STREET
ADELAIDE 5000
AUSTRALIA
PH 61 8 82125922
FAX 61 8 82310441
SALES@PREMIERART.COM.AU
WWW.PREMIERART.COM.AU

ABOUT THE AUTHOR

Growing up in my primary school years in the English Midlands, my first sewing and embroidery teacher thought I would never master any form of needlework. After failing on the very first task set, to knit a very uninspiring cotton dishcloth, the young Aquarian sought to prove her wrong.

Creativity has always been my driving force, with involvement in many types of crafts and sewing. I am self-taught in most of these, including ribbon embroidery. My hoped for training as an art teacher wasn't to happen, instead I qualified as a Registered Nurse, so for a number of years had little time for crafts and embroidery.

In the early 1970s I moved to Australia with my husband and two small daughters. I owned and ran a small craft shop in Port Lincoln on the west coast of South Australia. During this time our family grew to four, very talented, daughters. Our home was always creative chaos.

With a move to Adelaide in the mid 1980s, I soon became involved with craft groups and rediscovered embroidery. A thriving craft co-operative that sold a wide range of interesting crafts, occupied my time for quite a number of years.

I teach ribbon embroidery both in Adelaide and country areas with regular weekly classes and weekend retreats. Although bullion stitch is not one of my favourites, I contributed a number of the larger designs in the *A-Z Book of Bullion Stitches* in 1999.